# MODERN ARMOURED
# FIGHTING VEHICLES
## FROM 1946 TO THE PRESENT DAY

# MODERN ARMOURED FIGHTING VEHICLES
## FROM 1946 TO THE PRESENT DAY

AN ILLUSTRATED A–Z GUIDE TO AFVs OF THE WORLD,
FEATURING 76 VEHICLES AND 330 STUNNING PHOTOGRAPHS

**JACK LIVESEY**

**southwater**

This edition is published by Southwater
an imprint of Anness Publishing Ltd
Hermes House, 88–89 Blackfriars Road, London SE1 8HA
tel. 020 7401 2077; fax 020 7633 9499

www.southwaterbooks.com; www.annesspublishing.com

Anness Publishing has a new picture agency outlet for images for publishing, promotions
or advertising. Please visit our website www.practicalpictures.com for more information.

UK agent: The Manning Partnership Ltd, 6 The Old Dairy,
Melcombe Road, Bath BA2 3LR; tel. 01225 478444;
fax 01225 478440; sales@manning-partnership.co.uk

UK distributor: Grantham Book Services Ltd, Isaac Newton Way,
Alma Park Industrial Estate, Grantham, Lincs NG31 9SD;
tel. 01476 541080; fax 01476 541061; orders@gbs.tbs-ltd.co.uk

North American agent/distributor: National Book Network,
4501 Forbes Boulevard, Suite 200, Lanham, MD 20706;
tel. 301 459 3366; fax 301 429 5746; www.nbnbooks.com

Australian agent/distributor: Pan Macmillan Australia,
Level 18, St Martins Tower,
31 Market St,
Sydney, NSW 2000;
tel. 1300 135 113; fax 1300 135 103;
customer.service@macmillan.com.au

New Zealand agent/distributor: David Bateman Ltd,
30 Tarndale Grove, Off Bush Road,
Albany, Auckland;
tel. (09) 415 7664; fax (09) 415 8892

Publisher: Joanna Lorenz
Senior Managing Editor: Conor Kilgallon
Senior Editor: Felicity Forster
Copy Editor and Indexer: Tim Ellerby

Cover Design: Jonathan Davison
Designer: Design Principals
Editorial Reader: Jay Thundercliffe
Production Manager: Steve Lang

ETHICAL TRADING POLICY

At Anness Publishing we believe that business should be conducted in an ethical and ecologically sustainable way, with respect for the environment and a proper regard to the replacement of the natural resources we employ. As a publisher, we use a lot of wood pulp to make high-quality paper for printing, and that wood commonly comes from spruce trees. We are therefore currently growing more than 500,000 trees in two Scottish forest plantations near Aberdeen – Berrymoss (130 hectares/320 acres) and West Touxhill (125 hectares/305 acres). The forests we manage contain twice the number of trees employed each year in paper-making for our books. Because of this ongoing ecological investment programme, you, as our customer, can have the pleasure and reassurance of knowing that a tree is being cultivated on your behalf to naturally replace the materials used to make the book you are holding. Our forestry programme is run in accordance with the UK Woodland Assurance Scheme (UKWAS) and will be certified by the internationally recognized Forest Stewardship Council (FSC). The FSC is a non-government organization dedicated to promoting responsible management of the world's forests. Certification ensures forests are managed in an environmentally sustainable and socially responsible basis. For further information about this scheme, go to www.annesspublishing.com/trees.

A CIP catalogue record for this book is available from the British Library.

Previously published as part of a larger volume, *The World Encyclopedia of Armoured Fighting Vehicles*

1 3 5 7 9 10 8 6 4 2

**NOTE**
The nationality of each vehicle is identified in the relevant specification
box by the national flag that was current at the time of the vehicle's use.

PAGE 1: **Rapier Tracked SAM Vehicle.** PAGE 2: **SA-8b "Gecko" SAM Vehicle.**
PAGE 3: **BTR-60 Armoured Personnel Carrier.** PAGE 5: **AS90 155mm Self-Propelled Gun.**

# Contents

# Introduction

Armoured Fighting Vehicles (AFVs) form one of the most complex groups of machines to be found on a modern battlefield. Excluding the tank, the AFV encompasses a wide and diverse range of machines that are multi-tasking and multi-functional. They form the core of the armoured division and are found in greater numbers around the world than the tank, which they replace in some armies.

After an initial period of diverse and often unsuccessful development, AFVs became rationalized into three main types. These were the armoured car, which was the first of the AFVs to see action, the Self-Propelled Gun (SPG) and the Armoured Personnel Carrier (APC), both following on more slowly.

One of the most critical decisions involved with any proposed AFV development is the choice between wheels or tracks as the form of mobility. At first wheeled vehicles had very poor cross-country ability when compared with that of the fully-tracked tank. However, today this has largely been overcome and wheeled vehicle have very good cross-country ability, may be air-portable, and can be used in an urban area far more easily than tracked vehicles.

The armoured car as its name implies has always used wheels; however their primary reconnaissance role has from time to time been carried out by light tanks, which have excellent cross-country performance and improved protection but generally lower speeds than their wheeled counterparts. The SPG is usually mounted on tracks but wheeled SPGs have also been developed – a particular speciality of the Russians.

TOP: **The Marksman SPAAG (Self-Propelled Anti-Aircraft Gun) was developed by BAe Systems for the British Army but it was not taken into service. As yet it has only been sold to Finland.** ABOVE: **The LAV-25 8x8 APC is a copy of the Swiss MOWAG Piranha, one of the world's most successful armoured personnel carriers. The LAV-25 is built by General Motors of Canada and has been sold to many countries around the world, including the USA.**

The APC started life as little more than a battlefield taxi for the infantry, and was typified in World War II by vehicles with a combination of wheels and tracks, known as half-tracks. Being such a useful and versatile vehicle, APCs were very quickly adapted to fulfil other roles such as command, armoured ambulance, and supply functions.

The development of accurate artillery and the mass-production of the machine-gun spelt the end for horse-mounted cavalry. As a result the armoured car rapidly replaced the cavalry in the role of reconnaissance. It is now one of the main Armoured Reconnaissance Vehicles (ARVs) to be found on the battlefield. The ARV has to be well armed and armoured, and capable of travelling at relatively high speed. The main work of this vehicle is to serve as the eyes of the army well in advance of its own front-line. It relies on speed

ABOVE LEFT: **The Gepard Flakpanzer 1 emerged in the late 1960s as an indigenous SPAAG for the West German Army. The Contraves turret mounts twin 35mm/1.38in Oerlikon KDA cannon. The Gepard chassis is based on the Leopard 1 MBT.** TOP: **The Fox FV 721 armoured car entered service with the British Army in 1973 as a replacement for the Ferret armoured car. It is armed with a 30mm/1.18in RARDEN cannon which can destroy light armoured vehicles at 1,000m/3,281ft.** ABOVE: **The Commando M706 armoured car was built by Cadillac Gage for the US Army. Originally intended as an export vehicle for police forces around the world, it saw extensive service during the Vietnam War with both the South Vietnamese and US armies as a convoy escort vehicle.**

and agility to get out of trouble if observed by the opposing forces. However, as the destructive power of anti-tank guns has increased, armoured cars have become larger, exchanging some of their speed for increased crew protection.

The APC has undergone the greatest metamorphosis of all to emerge as the Infantry Fighting Vehicle (IFV). The APC started life as a vehicle with a lightly armoured open-topped box for transporting infantry to the edge of the fighting. From this position the infantry then had to leave the vehicle and attack the enemy on foot with support from the vehicle. In contrast, the modern IFV allows the infantry to attack from the safety of their vehicle that can fight its own way into the enemy position and then disgorge the troops.

Superficially the SPG shares many characteristics with the tank and this frequently causes the general public to confuse the two. Their role is to support tank attacks with high-explosive artillery rounds. Since the end of World War II guns have become increasingly more sophisticated and accurate and missiles are beginning to replace the gun in some cases.

This book contains a wide selection of armoured fighting vehicles from around the world dating from immediately post-World War II to the present day. The selection of machines concentrates on those that are of interest and importance and which particularly demonstrate the diversification of the AFV.

This book does not attempt to be definitive but aims to give the reader an insight into why the AFV plays such a crucial role in military forces around the world today.

# Key to flags

For the specification boxes, the national flag that was current at the time of the vehicle's use is shown.

| | |
|---|---|
| Brazil | The Netherlands |
| Canada | South Africa |
| Czechoslovakia | Switzerland |
| Eire (Republic of Ireland) | United Kingdom |
| France | United States |
| West Germany | USSR |

# The History of Modern Armoured Fighting Vehicles

In the 60 years since the end of World War II the AFV has undergone many transformations. This has resulted in a group of vehicles of great diversity, designed for a wide range of applications.

Foremost in the drive for innovation and evolution has been the ever-changing nature of conflict in the latter part of the 20th century and beyond. This has seen AFVs being deployed in both their traditional battlefield roles and in new areas such as international peacekeeping, anti-terrorism and civil policing.

The AFV has also benefited from developments in manufacturing methods and materials. AFVs are now constructed from composite materials, making them very light and fast, yet giving the crew adequate protection. This is combined with highly sophisticated weapons, communications and navigation systems.

The introduction of nuclear and chemical weapons to the modern battlefield has also placed a significant requirement on modern AFV design. AFVs now need to provide protection for their crews and infantry from these unseen threats. This is vital because it takes 20 days to produce a vehicle but 20 years to grow a soldier. The priority is clear.

LEFT: **The Soviet Frog-7 TEL taking part in a miltary parade. The rapid deployment and mobility of this weapons system was a key factor in its effectiveness.**

# The Cold War

World War II finished in 1945. The Cold War, which started in 1946 between the NATO countries (USA and most of Western Europe) and those of the Soviet-led Warsaw Pact, would last for some 45 years. The two sides never actually came to blows, each no doubt deterred by the military might of their opponents. The Cold War would see the greatest arms race in Man's history; it would cover land, sea, air and space. Money for research and development into better weapon systems was freely available at first, but with crippling debts from World War II, most countries had to drop out of the race leaving the Americans and the Soviet Union as the front runners.

The Soviets placed large numbers of men in highly mechanized units and machines along the border with Western Europe – the infamous "Iron Curtain". The idea was that the Soviets would launch an NBC (nuclear, biological or chemical) attack first, then the mechanized forces would flood through in a Blitzkrieg-style attack on the NATO forces.

The members of NATO decided to try for standardization throughout their armed forces. A large number of members could not afford to develop new weapons and so looked to

> "An iron curtain has descended across the Continent."
> Sir Winston Churchill, March 5, 1946

TOP: **An American cruise missile TEL system on exercise in Britain. The vehicle had a MAN Cat I AI 8x8 tractor unit and a separate trailer which carried four Tomahawk missiles. It had a crew of four.** ABOVE: **A Soviet Scud B missile system being driven to a site. The launch vehicle was known as the 9P117 and the MAZ-7310 LTM. It has a crew of four and can only carry one missile at a time.**

America to act as the main weapon supplier. Ammunition was standardized, and the same thing was done to vehicle types. The idea was that you developed one engine and chassis and then this basic vehicle filled many roles. In Britain, the 432 chassis was produced as a basic APC with 12 different models and an SPG. The Land Rover became a multipurpose vehicle, being produced in reconnaissance, anti-tank, signals and ambulance roles. In America, the M113 was produced and sold to over 40 different countries (not all members of NATO), with some 40 different types being created due to local modifications. Some models of both the 432 and the M113 were turned into anti-tank weapons. In the late 1950s and early 60s the guided missile started to make an appearance on the

ABOVE LEFT: A German Leopard passing an M113 APC. The troops are riding on the outside of the vehicle, which is a very common practice of infantry using this type of carrier. ABOVE RIGHT: A Lance missile is about to be launched from an M752 TEL. This vehicle uses many of the parts of the M113 APC. It has a crew of four and is still in service with many countries. LEFT: A column of Soviet BMP-1 IFVs crossing a river, demonstrating that it is fully amphibious. When this vehicle first entered service it gave NATO a real fright. It has a crew of three and carries an infantry section of eight men in the rear of the vehicle. BELOW: A Berlin Brigade British FV 432 APC. On the top of the vehicle is a wire basket for additional storage. To the rear of the basket is a yellow flashing light which is carried on military tracked vehicles when travelling on public roads. British troops are no longer based in Berlin.

battlefield. At the time this new lightweight weapon was supposed to sound the death knell of the Main Battle Tank (MBT). It could be mounted on just about any type of AFV and turn that vehicle into a tank killer. In the same way, the contemporary guided missile was expected to end the threat of fighter aircraft.

Vehicles and weapons were becoming very sophisticated and so required a higher degree of training for the troops who were to use the system in battle. In the West this weighted the balance in favour of professional volunteer armies. After World War II, America stopped conscription only to reintroduce it during the Vietnam War. Britain ceased conscription in 1962 and concentrated on developing a small but very professional army. This army would develop a very good reputation around the world and in 1982 would fight a war in the Falkland Islands that most of the world felt they could not win. Again during the Gulf War, Britain would demonstrate how professional and highly trained its armed forces were. The Soviet Union for the

most part stayed with a conscripted army, as it decided to make its weapons more basic and simpler to use. Consequently they were able to sell their weapons far and wide outside the Soviet Union and some of these have continued to be used long after becoming obsolete in the Cold War scenario.

Another major change in tactics and basic army doctrine was the introduction of the helicopter into service and its effect on military operations. The helicopter has changed the speed at which troops can be moved from one part of the battlefield to another. During the Vietnam War, the Americans fitted their transport helicopters with machine-guns and rockets, and this has now been taken one stage further with the development of the helicopter gunship. Heavy lift helicopters are also capable of moving artillery and light AFVs around the battlefield and newer vehicles are being developed to make the most of this capability.

With the collapse of the Soviet Union and the end of the Cold War in the early 1990s, some Warsaw Pact countries have joined NATO, and old enemies now work and train together.

LEFT: **British Saracen 6x6 APC.** This is a tropical version of the Saracen with raised engine intakes on the engine housing. The turret has been fitted with an additional four smoke dischargers.
BELOW: **Rhodesian mine-protected vehicle called the Leopard.** This is built using a Volkswagen beetle chassis. It has no fixed armament and relies on the small arms of the men inside the vehicle.

# The battlefield taxi with NBC and mine protection

Nuclear, Biological and Chemical (NBC) warfare is a new and terrifying type of war that has come to man with the onset of the Cold War. Open-topped vehicles offered little protection for the crew from this new type of warfare. At the same time a lot of time and money was being spent on training these men because armies after World War II were becoming smaller and more professional. Here was a great incentive to develop protection for vehicle crews and infantry as quickly as possible.

The first modern APCs in the Soviet armed forces were open-topped such as the BTR-152. They gave the crew very little protection from incoming fire or the weather and were not very different from what the Allied forces had used during World War II. By the early 1960s this mistake had been rectified by the Soviet designers and new vehicles such as the BTR-60

and the BMP-1 came on to the scene. The BTR-60 was no danger to the NATO forces, but the BMP-1 was a very different matter and frightened the life out of NATO commanders. The BTR-60 and the BMP-1 are both fully amphibious and have a full NBC system fitted to protect the crew of the vehicle and the infantry section being carried. The Soviet NBC system first draws the outside air into a multi-filter that removes all the dangerous agents, then passes it through a heater if necessary and then into the crew compartment. The air pressure in the vehicle is also kept several atmospheres higher than the outside pressure, which ensures no chemicals or other agents can leak into the vehicle through the side gun-ports.

The first British APCs, such as the Humber "Pig" and the Saracen, did not have any form of NBC protection for the crew or the infantry section. This fault was put right when the 432 came into service. The vehicle was fully NBC protected just as other more modern vehicles have continued to be to this day. The Americans took a very different approach with the M113 and only protected the vehicle crew of the driver and commander and two others. The other nine men in the vehicle have to use their own respirators. Even in a more modern vehicle like the Bradley there is no protection for the infantry in the back of the vehicle. Crews for the open SPGs like the M110 had no NBC protection at all except for their own personnel NBC clothing.

LEFT: **Soviet BMP-1 MICV.** This shows the back of the vehicle with the bulged rear doors, which is one of the major weaknesses of the vehicle as they contain fuel tanks. The low profile of the turret can be clearly seen and the very narrow tracks which give the vehicle a high ground pressure.

LEFT: **Two American M113 APCs. The driver's hatch is in the open position, with the vehicle's 12.7mm/50cal machine-gun beside it. The commander's position is to the rear of the machine-gun. The M113 has been sold to nearly 50 countries around the world and will remain in service for many years.**
BELOW: **An American M2 Bradley halted and debussing its infantry section. The great height of the vehicle shows up clearly here and is a major weakness of the vehicle. The M2 has had several upgrades to help improve its performance and armoured protection.**

The anti-tank mine has always been a problem for wheeled and tracked vehicles. Designers have tried to give wheeled vehicles some form of survivability by making these vehicles bigger with six or eight wheels so if one is destroyed the vehicle can still get the crew to a place of safety. In Zimbabwe and South Africa between 1972 and 1980 there was a proliferation of armoured vehicles designed to protect the occupants from mines. The main body was shaped to direct the blast from the mine down and away from the vehicle, as with the 5-ton Crocodile which could carry up to 18 men in the troop compartment. Vehicles such as the Hippo were designed with the main body of the vehicle raised up off the chassis and again shaped to direct the blast away from it. A Land Rover-based product Ojay was produced for the domestic market. In Russia the BTR-80 and 90 have been designed to operate with several wheels damaged or blown off. The Germans have also developed this system for their heavy wheeled vehicles like the Luchs and the Fuchs. The American M113 has a very weak floor. During the Vietnam War, a large number of men were injured riding in the vehicle, so the floor was covered with sandbags and the men remained on top until fired upon. The Russians had the same problem in Afghanistan with the BMP-1 and 2, and their crews also rode on top until attacked.

ABOVE: **Soviet troops climbing into the rear of a BMP-1. The eight-man infantry section sit back-to-back with the main fuel tank between them, and the rear doors also act as fuel tanks. As can be seen, Soviet mechanized infantry have very basic webbing and personal equipment.**

"The bullets entered our half-tracks and rattled around a little killing all inside."
General Omar Bradley to General George Patton (Kasserine Pass), 1942

LEFT: **British FV 432 APC travelling in convoy and at speed through a forest. The vehicle commander is standing up in his position giving instructions to the driver, who has his seat in the fully raised position. The hatches above the mortar are also in the open position.**
BELOW: **French AMX VCI armed with a 20mm/0.79in cannon and coaxial 7.62mm/0.3in machine-gun. This was an optional extra that could be fitted to the vehicle. An infantry section of ten men is carried in the rear of the vehicle, each man having his own firing port.**

# The birth of the Infantry Fighting Vehicle

Mechanized infantry tactics up till the late 1950s used the APC as a battlefield taxi, taking the infantry to the edge of the fighting. The infantry would then debus and go into action on foot. Both the British and the Americans were developing replacements for their ageing APCs, which resulted in 1960 with the Americans putting the M113 into production, followed in 1962 by the British with the 432, but these new vehicles would not herald any great change in tactics. The Soviets were also working on a new vehicle which would change infantry tactics for ever and which scared NATO commanders witless.

This new vehicle was the BMP-1 Infantry Fighting Vehicle (IFV). It was the first Soviet vehicle to be designed with the nuclear battlefield in mind from the start. The BMP-1 was one of the most significant innovations in AFV design in the latter half of the 20th century. Development started in the early 1960s, with trials commencing in 1964. In 1966, as the vehicle was about to be placed into production, the Soviet leader Nikita Khrushchev felt the vehicle was too expensive and that troops could be taken into battle far cheaper by the basic truck. Khrushchev was replaced as leader in the same year by Leonid Brezhnev who now rescinded the cancellation and allowed the BMP-1 to go into production. The BMP-1 was the first vehicle

that could take troops right into the engagement zone. The men inside could fire their weapons from the safety of the vehicle at first, and then when in a suitable position, the troops would debus and fight on foot with close support supplied by the BMP-1's gun. In a major change in tactics, only 8 men could be carried in the rear of the vehicle. They sat in two rows of four facing outwards, each man having a firing port for his own personal weapon. This vehicle was first seen by the Western powers at the Moscow May Day Parade in 1967.

NATO had to find away of combating this new threat. There was no way a new vehicle could be designed and developed from scratch, placed into production and then into service in the near future. The Germans were developing a multi-role chassis for a new family of vehicles including an IFV, the first prototypes of which were produced between 1961 and 1963. Eventually the vehicle went into production in 1970 and entered service with the German Army in 1971. Britain and America

> "The quickest and most effective way to exploit the success of the tank is by motorized infantry especially if the soldiers' vehicles are armoured and have complete cross country ability."
> General Heinz Guderian *Achtung – Panzer!,* 1937

were lagging far behind so they both went down the road of trying to turn the 432 and the M113 into IFVs from the APC. The Americans started development of the XM723 in 1972. In 1976, some changes were required to the basic vehicle out of which two vehicles would emerge: the XM2 IFV and the XM3 Cavalry Fighting Vehicle (CFV). The XM2 had a name change to the M2 Bradley and would enter service with the American Army in March 1983. In 1977, Britain started design and development of the MCV-80, which became the Warrior IFV, the idea being to replace most of the 3,000 432s in service with the Warrior. Orders were placed for 2,000 vehicles with the first entering service in 1987. With the ending of the Cold War in 1989 the order was cut back and the life span of the 432 has been extended by some 30 years, and the same has happened in America with the M2 Bradley and the M113.

ABOVE: **Soviet BTR-70 APC. This particular vehicle is not a standard infantry vehicle as it has several side hatches down the length of the vehicle. The trim vane can be seen in the stowed position under the nose of the vehicle.**

The BMP and the Bradley both have amphibious capability, but the British Warrior does not as it was felt it was not required. The real problem with these vehicles is that they are too heavy to be transported by air except in the largest transports. The Bradley and the Warrior both proved to be very reliable during the Gulf War and Operation "Iraqi Freedom", and have even taken on the role of light tank in some areas. New smaller versions of the IFV are under development so that they can fit into the air-portable Rapid Reaction Force.

ABOVE: **This British Warrior is stopped and is covering the infantry section that has debussed from the vehicle during an exercise. Only half of the infantry section can be seen.** LEFT: **A West German Marder MICV. The vehicle commander and driver have their hatches open. The turret is fitted with six smoke dischargers. The box on the side of the turret is a laser sight.** BELOW: **A column of M2 Bradley MICVs passing over a temporary pontoon bridge during an exercise in Germany. The vehicle commander and gunner are almost out of the turret helping to give the driver information on the vehicle's position. Each pontoon has a single crewman looking after the pontoon's station-keeping.**

# Playing catch-up

Armies around the world have from time to time found themselves in the position of having to play catch-up against an enemy that out of the blue produces a new vehicle. There are two options open: either produce your own version of the new vehicle, or convert some of your existing stock into something similar to what the enemy has produced. The AFV seems to be capable of adjustments to meet almost any threat or need. These range from conversions done in the field to overcome a local problem, to production-line enhancements to fill the gap until more specialized vehicles become available. Its adaptability is truly amazing.

During World War II, the engineering officer of the German Panzerjager unit 653 converted a few of his unarmed Bergepanther recovery vehicles into armed vehicles by fixing Panzer IV turrets on them. The Germans took a number of old tank chassis like the Panzer II and placed the PaK40 anti-tank gun on some of these vehicles. They also did a large number of conversions on captured vehicles, turning them into mobile anti-tank guns or SPGs. The French Lorraine Schlepper chassis was used for two conversions, one to a 105mm/4.13in SPG and one armed with a PaK40 anti-tank gun.

The Israeli Defence Force have for many years been the masters of the vehicle conversion, turning old or captured vehicles into something new that they could use. The L33 SPG is a prime example of these conversions. They took the very old Sherman tank chassis and placed a 155mm/6.1in gun mounted in a very large box structure the size of a house on it. Another conversion was the Ambutank, also based on a

Sherman tank chassis but with the engine moved forward. It was developed so that the Israelis could evacuate their wounded while under fire – the rear area has been turned into an ambulance capable of taking stretcher cases.

A number of World War II vehicles were put into action during the recent troubles between Bosnian and Serbian forces in the former Yugoslavia. One of these was the M36 tank destroyer with "spaced armour". The M36 was never designed to withstand modern weapons like the RPG7 anti-tank rocket, so wooden batons were placed down the side of the vehicle and the space between them filled in with concrete. This was

ABOVE: **British FV 432 APC armed with a 30mm/1.18in RARDEN cannon. Each mechanized British infantry battalion had 17 of these vehicles. This is the same two-man turret as that fitted to the Fox armoured car.** BELOW: **A 90mm/3.54in turret developed by Israel Defence Industries in 2004 to give the M113 a greater punch and extend its service life. This two-man turret has also been used to upgrade Chile's M24 Chaffee tanks.**

then covered in heavy rubber sheeting that used to be conveyer belting in a factory. The other major change was in the engine. The old American engine was removed and with a little adaptation a Soviet T55 tank engine was dropped into the same space.

When the Soviets unveiled the BMP-1 at the May Day Parade in 1967, the British and Americans had only just brought the 432 and the M113 into service a few years previously and so had to make do with what they had until new vehicles like the IFV could be developed. The 432 and the M113 had a large number of conversions performed on them, both to improve the firepower of the basic vehicle and to give additional support to an infantry attack. Britain has done a number of conversions to the 432 by putting RARDEN 30mm/1.18in gun turrets on the top of the vehicle, and some 432s have been fitted with the Swingfire anti-tank missile to give the vehicle the ability to kill tanks. The Ferret armoured car was also fitted with two Swingfire missiles, one on each side

ABOVE LEFT: **British FV 432 APC fitted with a 120mm/4.72in Wombat Recoilless Rifle. The gun can be fired from the vehicle or dismounted, but the vehicle only carries 14 rounds of ammunition.** ABOVE: **American M113A2 Improved TOW Vehicle (ITV). This is a basic APC but fitted with the Raytheon TOW ATGW (Anti-Tank Guided Weapon). The vehicle carries ten missiles but no infantry.**

of the turret. Some 60,000 M113 vehicles have been produced since it went into production, a small number of which were converted on the production line, while others were converted by the different countries that bought them. The Australians at first placed old British Saladin armoured car turrets on some of their M113s and turned them into close-support vehicles. These have now been upgraded with the British Scorpion 76mm/2.99in turret. The RARDEN 30mm/1.18in turret and the British Fox armoured car turret is also capable of being fitted as an upgrade. The Swiss have fitted the 20mm/0.79in Hagglunds turret to some of their M113, and this conversion is also for sale to other M113 users.

LEFT: **A French AMX-30 chassis is used to mount the Euromissile Roland SAM system. The turret is in the raised position. The vehicle carries two missiles in the launcher and eight in the vehicle.** ABOVE: **American M163 Vulcan SPAAG. The vehicle has a crew of four but the turret is only a one-man operation. Developed by General Dynamics and entering service in 1965, the American Army had 671 of these vehicles in service by 1987.**

# Peacekeeping around the world

In the last 35 years, armed forces around the world have found themselves having to undertake the role of riot-control forces and to do internal security operations that they have not been trained or equipped for. This has led to the development of many special vehicles that can protect the men using them and yet be non-confrontational.

Full tracked vehicles such as the British 432, Warrior and Challenger tank are not suitable for this job, as they are very expensive to operate and maintain compared to a wheeled vehicle. Tracked vehicles like tanks and IFVs have very poor manoeuvrability in built-up areas, poor observation for the driver and commander, and can cause headlines in newspapers and on TV of "tanks on the streets". AFVs have proved their adaptability in these situations, with some conversions. The vision blocks of the vehicle have to be fitted with wipers and a cleaning fluid dispenser for a form of paint remover. Diesel is the preferred fuel for internal security vehicles as it does not burn as easily as petrol, and diesel engines have more economic fuel consumption.

When the "Troubles" started in Northern Ireland in 1969, the British Army had disposed of almost all its Humber 1-ton 4x4 wheeled APCs which were being sold off for scrap, to vehicle collectors or to the Belgian Army. These were all bought back at an increased cost and put back into service, and some of the 6x6 Saracen APCs were also sent to Northern Ireland.

TOP: **British Warrior MICV armed with the 30mm/1.18in RARDEN cannon. All three of the crew can be seen. They have placed light blue UN covers over their helmets so they are easily visible and the vehicle has been painted white.**
ABOVE: **British Ferret Mk 2 in UN colours. The British Army has taken a full and active part in United Nations peacekeeping since World War II.**

The Humber 1-ton APC is better known as the "Pig" because it was a pig to drive. When in 1972 the IRA managed to acquire armour-piercing bullets, the Pig could not protect the troops from this new type of ammunition. All 500 Pigs were upgraded with better armour and armoured glass was put in the vision slits. Some Pigs were further converted with large gate-like structures covered in wire mesh that were attached to the

Warrior

RIGHT: **The nickname for UN troops is the Blue Helmets, and their vehicles are always painted white so there can be no confusing the fact that these men and women are on peacekeeping duties.**
BELOW: **British Saxon Patrol. This vehicle was developed to replace ageing security vehicles such as the Humber "Pig" in Northern Ireland. The Saxon has been fitted with "wings" – riot-control screens that can be deployed from side of the vehicle.**

> "Our country is going to be what our people have proclaimed
> it must be – the Arsenal of Democracy."
> Franklin D. Roosevelt, April 1916

ABOVE: **Dutch Army AIFV in UN colours. The vehicle is an improved M113A1 and entered service in 1975 with the Dutch Army, who have bought 880. The AIFV has a crew of three and can carry an infantry section of seven men.**
BELOW: **British Warrior on sentry duty at the city boundary of Sarajevo in Bosnia. A large number of NATO forces were sent to the Balkans during the break-up of Yugoslavia to act as peacekeepers.**

sides of the vehicle and then swung out to give the troops protection from bottles, bricks and stones. This winged appearance gave rise to the name "Flying Pig".

South Africa has developed a special internal security vehicle in the Buffel. It has very high ground clearance, a V-shaped body to deflect the explosive force from mines, and a steel roof that can be folded down. The downside of this vehicle is that it has a very high centre of gravity and so can tip over when taking corners too fast or trying to cross rough ground. In Britain, the Saxon has been developed to be used in urban areas. Based on a Bedford truck chassis, the vehicle has a good ground clearance and has been sold to several other countries as an internal security vehicle.

The Shorts company of Northern Ireland has been building an internal security vehicle called the Shorland for many years. It is based on the Land Rover chassis and has been sold to some 40 countries, proving to be very cost effective and reliable. In America, the Cadillac company have produced the Commando III that is in use with most police departments in the USA and the National Guard.

In the former USSR, no special internal security vehicles were built. If there was a riot or demonstration then the police would work alongside the army, and standard armoured vehicles, including tanks, would be used against the unarmed public, as happened in Hungary in 1956 and later in Poland.

The East Germans did produce an armoured water cannon for the police and internal security forces. The vehicle was the SK-2, based on the G5 6x6 heavy truck, which was used in large numbers by the East German Army. The water cannon, with a range of 70m/230ft, was mounted on the roof in a small turret with a 360-degree traverse. It was reloaded by driving the vehicle over a water main, opening a trapdoor in the floor, and lowering a pipe to connect the vehicle to the water supply, taking 10 minutes to refill the water tanks in the vehicle.

# Air mobility

In 1930 the Soviets formed the world's first parachute force and commanders have tried ever since to give airborne troops an armoured capability. Trying to fit a tank into a transport aircraft has always been very difficult, due to the weight and size of the vehicle. During World War II, the Allies used Horsa and Hamilcar gliders to move heavy equipment to the landing zone of the parachute troops. These gliders could only carry small light vehicles such as the Jeep and the Universal Carrier (which was used to tow 6-pound anti-tank guns) until the British developed a small light tank. This was called the Tetrarch and was armed with a 2-pound gun and capable of being carried by the Hamilcar. The Germans meanwhile concentrated on powered flight and built the largest transport aircraft of the war that could carry 3-ton trucks and light tanks such as the Panzer II. After World War II, larger transport aircraft with large rear loading doors came into service with other armies, but as tanks have grown in size and weight they could still not be carried. Even today the only aircraft capable of carrying a Main Battle Tank (MBT) are the American C5 Galaxy or the Soviet AN 124 and even these aircraft, the biggest in the world, can only carry two MBTs. Since the Vietnam War, the heavy lift types of helicopter have changed the way troops, guns, vehicles and supplies move around the battlefield.

With the ending of the Cold War and the break up of the Soviet Union, the type of warfare that modern armies are training to fight has changed. Long gone are the massed ranks of Warsaw Pact tanks facing the NATO forces on the ground,

TOP: **An American M551 Sheridan light tank being loaded on to a C130 transport aircraft. This was designed to equip the American airborne divisions, but withdrawn from service after only five years due to its vulnerability.** ABOVE: **A Willys Jeep being unloaded from a British Horsa glider in front of General Montgomery. The bumpers have been cut down and all the tie-downs and handles have been removed.**

and the battlefield of Western Europe has melted away to be replaced by the worldwide battlefield. Soldiers and their equipment have to be able to move very quickly and respond to a changing enemy with either low-technology weapons or good weapons but poorly trained operatives, or a mix of both. Troops used to be sent to the theatre of operations by aircraft with their heavy equipment following on in ships, but now soldiers and heavy equipment can be transported by air to theatre.

Vehicles like the British CVR(T) Scorpion can be airlifted to any part of the world and can then be slung under helicopters like the Chinook and delivered to the front line ready for battle. These fast light vehicles now carry a big punch and, being part of a fully integrated force, can respond to most situations that they come across. The sheer speed that commanders can now get troops into a theatre does not give the enemy time to construct defences or build up ground forces and supplies. Also, as the response time is now hours and not days, the local defence forces stand a better chance of holding the attackers at bay until reinforcements and AFVs arrive.

AFVs can also be delivered direct to the battlefield by heavy-lift aircraft from which the vehicles can be delivered by parachute or Low Altitude Parachute Extraction System (LAPSE). This technique allows an aircraft such as the Hercules to come in very low and fast and deliver the tanks that are tied on to special air drop sledges. The Soviet Union has experimented with this system and others. One system they tried out was fitting an airborne AFV like the BMD to an air landing platform, with rockets fitted to the underneath and the crew inside the vehicle. The platform would be steadied on leaving the aircraft by a small chute, and a weighted rope would hang down from the platform. On striking the ground the rope would set off the retro rockets which would slow the descent of the platform and give the crew and the AFV a safe landing. Perhaps not surprisingly, the Soviets lost a number of men in these trials.

With more and more armies turning to rapid deployment forces, the heavy MBT is being cut back in numbers and replaced by lighter, faster and more agile light tanks or AFVs. Could this be the end of the MBT?

TOP: **French Leclerc MBT being loaded on to a heavy transport C5 aircraft. The major problems with vehicles like this are the weight of the vehicle and the size of the transport aircraft required to move them by air.** ABOVE LEFT: **A Willys Jeep inside an American WACO glider. The front bumper has been shortened and only one headlight is fitted. The vehicle is shackled to the steel frame of the glider and only just fits inside.** ABOVE: **German Wiesel air-portable light tank inside a CH-53G heavy-lift helicopter. The crew of the vehicle varies between two and five, depending on its designated role. The German Army have some 400 of these vehicles in service.** LEFT: **Soviet BMD-1 airborne combat vehicle. The turret has been covered and the main parachute is fitted to the rear deck of the vehicle. Originally the crew were in the vehicle when it left the aircraft but they now drop separately.**

# The multi-role family of vehicles

Long gone are the days of developing new vehicles from scratch, with new engines, chassis and weapons. These are very expensive, take a long time to come into service and require a lot of testing and training of new crews. World War II would see a new type of development where the vehicle "family" becomes more important. In Britain, the Churchill tank became the basic chassis for a number of new vehicles that would be known as the "Funnies". In the USA, several new vehicles such as the M10 and the M40, were based on the Sherman. The Germans turned the Panzer IV into a family of vehicles. Its well-tried and tested chassis gave rise to vehicles like the Hummel, Nashorn and Sturmgeschutz. The Soviets were a little behind on the idea of creating a basic chassis for several vehicles but the T-34 was used for several different vehicles including the SU100.

With the start of the Cold War and the birth of NATO with its ideas of standardization, the concept of a basic family of AFVs was born. In Britain the 432 was under development and would be produced in 19 variations, not including the SPG. In 1970

the CVR(T) Scorpion started its production run. This would lead to a new and revolutionary family of tracked vehicles that are capable of going were tanks cannot, and filling many of the MBT roles. Due to the very low ground pressure of the vehicle (less than an infantryman's foot in a size nine boot), this vehicle can even get to places on the battlefield where a soldier cannot. In the Falklands War of 1982, I watched a Scorpion come across a peat bog. The vehicle stopped and the commander jumped down, only to sink up to his knees while the CVR(T) sat on the top of the soft spongy ground. The CVR(T) is also the backbone of the Rapid Deployment Force as two can fit into a Hercules C-130 transport aircraft.

In the early 1960s, the Americans developed the M113 that would be produced in larger numbers than any other AFV since World War II with over 60,000 being built. It has been sold to 36 different countries around the world and there are 40 different variations on the basic vehicle chassis. These include bridge layers, flamethrowers, command, and anti-aircraft vehicles. The M113 has been in service for 40 years and it

> "The full power of an army can be exerted only when all its parts act in close combination."
> British Field Service Regulations, Part 1, 1909

ABOVE LEFT: **A line-up of British Spartan APCs. The cupola hatch opens to the rear and side and is the vehicle commander's position. The ambulance version of the Spartan family is called the Samaritan.** ABOVE: **British Spartan (FV 103) with Milan system on the rear of the vehicle. There are four of these vehicles per battalion. The vehicle has a narrow hull, blunt nose and a large sloping glacis plate. Two clusters of four smoke dischargers are mounted on the front.** LEFT: **Two British Spartan vehicles at speed in the desert during the Gulf War of 1991. All the personal kit of the crew and infantry in the vehicle has been stowed on the outside of the vehicle. Temporary storage boxes have also been fitted to the front of the vehicle.**

is expected to remain in service for many more years with the American Army and many of its customers. For most of its life, the US Marine Corps has had older and inferior equipment to the army. Now with the new Piranha Light Armoured Vehicle (LAV) they have a vehicle that will take them well into the future. The LAV has been developed into a family of vehicles that will remain at the forefront of future tactical development in both the US Army and Marine Corps for many years.

The French have produced several very good families of vehicles such as the AMX VCI. This is based on the very successful AMX-13 light tank chassis and has been in production since 1956. The early versions had an open machine-gun position on the top of the vehicle. By 1960, this had been replaced by a proper machine-gun turret and so could be regarded as the very first IFV. It has been sold to 10 different countries and produced in 12 different variations on the basic vehicle. The AMX VCI is now being replaced in the French Army by the AMX-10P that has so far been developed into ten variations on the basic IFV.

The former Soviet Union has in the past made several families of AFVs, which can be found in service all over the world. These vehicles, such as the BRDM, have been in service since 1960 but because of their basic design and simplicity of maintenance have been sold on to various Third World countries, and many remain in service today.

The AFV family of vehicles has proved an excellent idea and has given military commanders more options and a new flexibility in their tactical deployment of equipment and logistics on the battlefield.

TOP: **The Samaritan, like the other vehicles in the family, has no personal kit storage inside the vehicle, so in this case it is stored on the roof. The running gear can be clearly seen with the driving wheel at the front and the five large road wheels.**

ABOVE: **The British Striker SP ATGW (FV 102) launching a Swingfire missile. The rear launcher box is in the raised firing position, and holds five missiles. A further ten can be carried in the vehicle.**

LEFT: **The mother of the CVR(T) family is the Scorpion light tank. The three-man crew can be seen in their positions, with their personal kit stored on the outside of the vehicle. The turret is armed with a 76mm/2.99in main gun and coaxial 7.62mm/0.3in machine-gun.**

# The future

It takes a very brave or very foolish person to predict the future. Time and time again such predictions have been proved wrong and the history of the development of AFVs has plenty of examples of such mistakes. In the 1950s the new guided anti-tank missile was going to make the battlefield a no-go area for the MBT yet the tank is still, at present, king of the battlefield in spite of this.

Armies around the world are undergoing major changes and restructuring at this time. There now seems to be no need for the old heavy tank formations that used to be lined up in Europe like great armoured juggernauts. In Britain, army units are being amalgamated to form bigger and more flexible units. The heavy tank regiments armed with the Challenger MBT are being cut back in number and replaced by the lighter CVR(T) type of vehicle. The British Army is one of the few in the world that has its light armoured fighting vehicles still mounted on full tracks, as most of the world's armies are going over to the cheaper all-wheeled vehicle.

In 1999 General Eric Shinseki, the United States Army Chief of Staff, outlined a plan to reorganize the army into new types of units that could deal with future deployments better. The new units will be called Objective Forces and will be in

TOP: **American Multiple Launch Rocket System (MLRS) firing a salvo of missiles. This system was first tried in battle during the Gulf War of 1991. The large back blast from the missile can clearly be seen, but with a range of 30km/ 18.6 miles, it is not a problem.** ABOVE: **The MOWAG Piranha has become a very successful vehicle, being built in several countries around the world and in service with many others. It is expected to remain in service for the next 30 years.**

place by 2010, equipped with new all-wheeled Future Combat Vehicles (FCV). These vehicles will be produced in prototype form by 2005; they must be able to fit into a Hercules C-130 transport aircraft and must not weigh more than 20 tons. The armoured protection has to be as good, if not better, than the M1 Abrams MBT with full NBC protection. Another part of the plan is to form an interim force that will use existing wheeled vehicles and will be of brigade size. The brigade will have to be fully air-portable and be able to deploy anywhere in the world within 96 hours. A full division will have 120 hours to do the same. The vehicle chosen to equip the interim force is the LAV III which will be built by General Motors and it has already been

> "Infantry is the arm which in the end wins battles. To enable it to do so the cooperation of the other arms is essential."
> British Field Service Regulations, 1924

LEFT: **Under development is the Stormer SPAAM which has the Rapier missile system fitted to the rear of the vehicle. The Stormer is just entering British service and is a larger version of the Spartan CVR(T).**
BELOW: **Soviet BTR-80 BREM. This is the engineers' support vehicle and the turret has been fitted with a 3,048kg/3-ton "A"-frame. Behind the crane is storage for spare wheels and other heavy equipment. The BTR-80 is expected to remain in service for many years to come.**

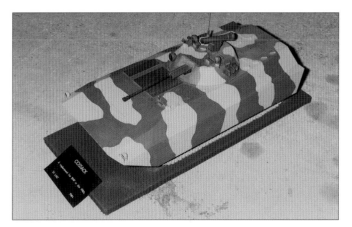

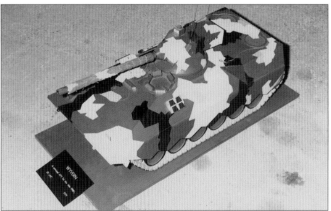

decided to create 10 variations of the basic vehicle. One of the reasons the LAV III has been selected is its top speed of 97kph/60mph, which means it can have a convoy speed of 64kph/40mph against tracked vehicles that have a convoy speed of 40kph/25mph. Over a century ago, Colonel Davidson suggested the formation of a cavalry unit using nothing but wheeled vehicles. Now the Americans feel the time is right for its formation.

Designers are looking at new propellants for munitions, as these at present take up a lot of space in the vehicle. If you can place more munitions in the vehicle then it can remain in action longer and logistic problems of rearming a vehicle decrease. One of the propellants the scientists are working on is liquid explosive, which would be injected into the breach of a gun once the warhead had been loaded. This will increase the space in the vehicle for more warheads and would make the use of automatic loaders a far better option. This will also either remove a crew member or free him for other duties in the vehicle. This offers new design possibilities.

Far more countries are beginning to develop their own wheeled AFVs, using basic truck chassis that can be bought "off the shelf" from many manufacturers. These might not have the sophistication of vehicles like the LAV III, but a high level of sophistication is not always required or desirable. Brazil used to be a major importer of AFVs but now it has started producing its own vehicles such as the EE-11 and is actively trying to sell them on the world market.

For the present the tank remains the king of the battlefield, but for how long? The AFV is now beginning to carry the punch of the Abrams MBT, can deliver a wide variety of munitions on to a target and get a high proportion of rounds on target first time to guarantee a kill.

ABOVE MIDDLE: **A development model of a Wyvern which was intended to be a principle AFV in the late 1990s. As yet, it has not made a public appearance, but it does show the trend for smaller lighter vehicles that can be moved by air.**
ABOVE: **A possible development model for a future BMP-3 called Cossack. The body of the vehicle has cleaner lines for better performance in the water, but it still looks large and too heavy to be air-portable.**

# A–Z of Modern Armoured Fighting Vehicles 1946 to the Present Day

With the beginning of the Cold War, an arms race started all around the world. Various weapons were rushed into development as military theory changed – such as the suggestion that the tank would become obsolete and would be replaced by the missile carrier. The armoured car remained a firm military favourite until 1970 when a number of armies replaced them with light tanks. Now, however, the armoured car has been revived and functions again as the eyes of armoured and infantry divisions. The self-propelled gun was developed further and has now become a very sophisticated weapons system with extremely long ranges that can reach far into the enemy's rear. Its modern mobility means the guns can use "shoot and scoot" tactics.

The infantry carrier has undergone the greatest metamorphosis of any vehicle type. In the early 1950s, carriers were open-topped vehicles with a single machine-gun. They then became "battlefield taxis" carrying the infantry to the battlefield in fully armoured vehicles with overhead protection. The latest infantry fighting vehicles take troops into the heart of the fighting while providing them with close support.

LEFT: **Fox armoured car.**

LEFT: **A 2S1 in a two-tone camouflage scheme. The driver and vehicle commander are in their positions with their hatches open. The driver has no physical contact with the turret crew. On the barrel behind the muzzle brake is the fume extractor.**

ABOVE: **A battery of 2S1 SPGs taking part in a parade to commemorate the November Revolution. The 2S1 was given the name "Gvozdika" (Carnation) by the Soviet Army. When it entered service, the 2S1 was first issued to BMP-equipped units.**

# 2S1 122mm Self-Propelled Gun

During the period when Khrushchev was in power in the Soviet Union from 1955–64, the armed forces were forced in the direction of nuclear weapons resulting in the demise of a number of basic weapon systems such as the SPG. When Leonid Brezhnev took over as the Soviet leader following Khrushchev's removal, it was realized that basic weapons development was lagging far behind those that NATO (the North Atlantic Treaty Organization) could deploy. In 1965, the GRAU (Gun Development Department) laid down a requirement for new conventionally tubed artillery, both towed and self-propelled. At this time NATO could field three main types of SPG, the M109, M110 and the Abbot, and had developed an excellent counter-battery fire technique based around these guns. With the development of improved artillery location radars the NATO guns could target the Soviet artillery very quickly, and with the new and improved ammunition at NATO's disposal, Soviet towed gun crews were very vulnerable.

The Soviet ground forces received several new guns in the 1960s. One was the D-30 122mm/4.8in towed gun and this was later mounted on a tracked chassis. Development of this vehicle started in the late 1960s and it was given the codename of "izdeliye 26". The chassis was developed by the GAVTU (Main Auto-transport Directorate) and was based on the MT-LB armoured transporter that was developed to replace the AT-P light artillery tractor. Production started in 1971 at the Karkov Tractor Plant, under the designation 2S1 Gvozdika (Carnation). The gun itself was a development of the 122mm/4.8in D-30, the main difference being the muzzle brake which on the 2S1 had a double baffle. The vehicle normally has a crew of four but when emplaced for a sustained fire role the crew is increased to six with the addition of two extra ammunition handlers. The gun can fire the full range of Soviet 122mm/4.8in ammunition to a maximum range of 15.2km/9.4 miles. The 2S1 carries 40 rounds of ammunition in the fighting compartment.

The 2S1 is fully amphibious and only takes a few minutes to be made ready to enter the water. The hull is boat-shaped and is very large, the bulky hull being necessary to provide enough buoyancy to allow the 2S1 to float. The vehicle uses its tracks to propel it through the water and a set of swim vanes are attached at the rear of the tracks to provide some form of steering. The driver is positioned right at the front of the vehicle on the left-hand side and his only contact with the fighting compartment is by internal intercom. The engine is placed alongside the driver, while the main air intake for the engine

LEFT: **A group of 2S1 vehicles demonstrating its amphibious capability. The vehicle commander is acting as the eyes for the driver who can see nothing from his position.**

LEFT: **A 2S1 in an artillery scrape and under a camouflage net. The driver's front visor is in the open position. Next to the driver's position is the access hatch to the clutch and compressed air system.** ABOVE: **A cut-away view of the 2S1. In the front of the vehicle is the compressed air unit and clutch, next is the driver's compartment, then the engine, followed by the main turret area and finally ammunition storage.**

is behind him. The gun is mounted in a turret at the rear of the vehicle and has a very low profile that has the appearance of an upside-down frying pan. The turret can be traversed through 360 degrees and is electrically powered or may be manually turned if necessary. The suspension is pneumatic and can be raised or lowered depending on the terrain that the vehicle is traversing. The vehicle is normally fitted with 400mm/15.7in wide tracks, but these can be replaced by 670mm/26.4in tracks to allow for better operation in snow or over soft ground.

The 2S1 chassis was used for a number of command vehicles, designated ACRV (Armoured Command and Reconnaissance Vehicle) and were attached to a number of SPG batteries. The ACRV-1 had a taller body, with the driver

at the front and the vehicle commander next to him and accommodation in the rear for four men. There was a fixed circular cupola on the roof with a single large hatch which was fitted with a 12.7mm/0.5in machine-gun. All versions of the 2S1 and the gun vehicle were equipped with a full NBC system.

The 2S1 was first seen in 1974 at a military parade in Poland, but had been in service for at least a year before this sighting. It was issued to Motor Rifle and Tank Divisions to replace the towed 122mm/4.8in guns. Each division had six 2S1 batteries attached to it, and each battalion had eighteen guns, divided between three batteries. Not surprisingly, given its adaptability and performance, it is still in service in many parts of the world today.

LEFT: **The engine grill can be seen in front of the turret. The grill on the back of the turret is for the air filtration unit that is mounted in the rear of the turret.**

### 2S1 122mm SPG

**Country:** USSR
**Entered service:** Approximately 1973
**Crew:** 4 plus 2 extra loaders
**Weight:** 15,951kg/15.7 tons
**Dimensions:** Length – 7.26m/23ft 10in
　　　Height – 2.73m/8ft 11in
　　　Width – 2.85m/9ft 4in
**Armament:** Main – 2A31 122mm/4.8in gun
　　　Secondary – Small arms
**Armour:** Maximum – 20mm/0.79in
**Powerplant:** YaMZ 238N V8 220kW/300hp
　　　diesel engine
**Performance:** Speed – Road 61kph/38mph;
　　　Water 4.5kph/2.8mph
　　　Range – 500km/311 miles

LEFT: **The muzzle brake has been covered by a canvas bag to stop dust and debris from entering the barrel while on the move. These vehicles belong to the East German Army, here seen in the Berlin area. This vehicle is fitted with an entrenching blade on the front of its hull.**

# 2S3 152mm Self-Propelled Gun

The development of this vehicle can be traced back to the end of World War II and the programmes of the Gorlitskiy design bureau based at the Uraltransmash plant at Sverdlovsk (now called Ekaterinberg) in 1949. Surprisingly, these designs were simply shelved and never went in to production. In 1965, some of the designs were resurrected and the first of these was the Obiekt 120 or SU-152. This was first modified in the early 1960s as the Obiekt 123 which became the SA-4 Ganef air defence missile system and was based on a 1949 chassis design. The Obiekt 120 was developed into a turreted self-propelled gun using the M-69 152mm/5.98in gun. This vehicle had a fully automatic loading system. A small number of these vehicles were built and put on trial but they were not accepted for service. In the late 1960s the Obiekt 303 was developed. This was another turreted self-propelled gun but used the 2A33 152mm/5.98in howitzer which was a development of the D-20 152mm/5.98in towed gun. In 1971 the Obiekt 303 was accepted for service in the Soviet Army and was renamed the 2S3 Akatsiya (Acacia).

The 2S3 is of an all-welded construction with thin armour that just about provides bullet and shrapnel protection to the crew (though not at close quarters) and is equipped with a dozer blade on the front for making its own field scrape. The driver has a compartment in the front of the vehicle with no direct contact with the rest of the crew in the fighting compartment. The engine is mounted next to the driver, and is a multi-fuel engine that normally uses diesel fuel but can in an emergency use other fuels for a short time. The vehicle is fitted with a full NBC system. Behind the engine and driver is the fighting compartment which takes up half the space in the vehicle. The turret can be traversed through 360 degrees,

ABOVE: **These 2S3 vehicles have just finished firing as evidenced by the dust created from the back-blast that is still settling. These vehicles were known as "Akatsiya" (Acacia) and they became the mainstay of Soviet mobile artillery.**

and the commander's cupola can be fitted with an anti-aircraft heavy machine-gun.

The gun was modernized twice in the 18 years of production. The first improvement, known as the 2S3M, came out in 1975 when the design of the autoloader was improved which increased the rate of fire of the vehicle. The second improvement, the 2S3M1, came out in 1987, with better communications and new sighting equipment for the gun. Normally there is a crew of four men on the 2S3, but in a sustained fire role two extra loaders can be placed outside the vehicle to load ammunition through two small hatches in the rear of the vehicle. The gun can fire all the Soviet types of 152mm/5.98in ammunition including nuclear shells, rocket-propelled shells (which give the gun a range of 30km/

18.6 miles) and precision-guided rounds such as the Krasnapol laser projectile. The normal rate of fire for this weapon is between three and four rounds per minute, but this cannot be sustained for long. The normal rate of fire in a sustained role is one round per minute, which means that the gun carries less than one hour's worth of ammunition, there being 46 rounds stored in the vehicle.

The 2S3 replaced the towed D-1 152mm/5.98in howitzer regiments in Motor Rifle Divisions. The new self-propelled 2S3 regiments consisted of eighteen vehicles divided into three batteries of six guns. In the tank regiments, the 2S3 replaced one battalion of 122mm/4.8in guns and gave the tank regiments greater firepower in the close-support role. This vehicle has also replaced a number of guns in the artillery divisions. The 2S3 is the second most common gun in the Soviet Army after the 2S1 and there were 2,012 in service in the western Soviet bloc in 1991, just prior to the break up of the Soviet Union. The 2S3 is now being replaced in the Russian Army by the new 2S19, but the 2S3 can still be found in service in 14 countries around the world. The Czechs were the only Soviet bloc country not to take the 2S3 as they had developed the wheeled 152mm/5.98in DANA self-propelled gun.

ABOVE: **Two East German 2S3 SPGs taking part in a November Parade in East Berlin. On the end of the barrel is a large double-baffle muzzle brake. There is also a fume extractor on the barrel.** BELOW LEFT: **When the 2S3 is being used in the sustained fire role then an ammunition vehicle can be parked at its rear and, using the two hatches in the lower rear hull, ammunition can be passed into the gun.**

ABOVE: **This vehicle has been painted up in a two-tone camouflage pattern. The commander's cupola has been fitted with a machine-gun.** BELOW LEFT: **An entrenching blade is fitted under the front of the 2S3, which allows the vehicle to dig its own firing scrape. The driver and vehicle commander are in their positions.**

## 2S3 152mm SPG

**Country:** USSR
**Entered service:** 1972
**Crew:** 4 plus 2 extra loaders
**Weight:** 27,940kg/27.5 tons
**Dimensions:** Length – 8.4m/27ft 7in
　　　　　Height – 3.05m/10ft
　　　　　Width – 3.25m/10ft 8in
**Armament:** Main – 2A33 152mm/5.98in howitzer
　　　　　Secondary – 7.62mm/0.3in PKT machine-gun
**Armour:** Maximum – 20mm/0.79in
**Powerplant:** V-59 12-cylinder 382kW/520hp multi-fuel engine
**Performance:** Speed – 60kph/37mph
　　　　　Range – 500km/311 miles

LEFT: **The 2S5 uses the same hull and chassis as the 2S3. The travel lock is mounted on the top of the driver's cupola. When operating the gun, the crew are very exposed. This vehicle was developed to improve the mobility of the towed 2A36.**

# 2S5 152mm Self-Propelled Gun

One of the last self-propelled guns of the first generation of mechanized artillery vehicles to enter service with the Soviet Army was the 2S5 Giatsint (Hyacinth). Development commenced in the early 1970s and the vehicle started life as the Obiekt 307, being a marriage of the Uraltransmash chassis as used for the 2S3 and the 2A36 towed 152mm/5.98in gun.

The 2S5 is of an all-welded construction, and the main body of the vehicle has just 15mm/0.59in of armour. The crew of five are very exposed when operating the weapon as they are out in the open behind the gun except for the gun layer, who is seated on the left, again in the open but with a small shield in front of him. The driver sits in the front on the left of the vehicle, while behind the driver is the vehicle and gun commander,

whose cupola is fitted with a machine-gun. Alongside them on the right of the vehicle is the compartment for the diesel and multi-fuel engine. The gun crew travel in a small compartment in the rear of the vehicle which is fitted with roof hatches for them. The gun is mounted on the roof at the rear of the vehicle, while to the left of the gun is storage for 30 warheads mounted on a carousel and on the other side of the vehicle are the 30 propellant charges. Crew fatigue is kept to a minimum by the use of a semi-automatic loading system. There is a large recoil spade on the rear of the vehicle and a small dozer blade is fitted to the front for removing small obstacles and making gun scrapes.

The 2S5 entered service in 1974, but was not identified by NATO until 1981. It

ABOVE: **The recoil spade on the rear of the 2S5 is in the raised position. The gun crew are entering the crew compartment in the middle of the vehicle, with the driver up front.**

replaced a number of towed guns in the heavy artillery brigades at army level. The 2S5 can be brought into action in just three minutes and a battery of six guns can put 40 rounds of ammunition in the air before the first one has landed. It is now being replaced by the 2S19.

RIGHT: **The entrenching spade can be seen under the front of the vehicle. The slotted muzzle brake of the gun can also be clearly seen. Mounted in the open like this, the gun is susceptible to damage.**

### 2S5 152mm SPG

**Country:** USSR
**Entered service:** 1974
**Crew:** 5 plus 2 extra loaders
**Weight:** 28,956kg/28.5 tons
**Dimensions:** Length – 8.33m/27ft 4in
　　Height – 2.76m/9ft 1in
　　Width – 3.25m/10ft 8in
**Armament:** Main – 2A37 152mm/5.98in gun
　　Secondary – 7.62mm/0.3in PKT machine-gun
**Armour:** Maximum – 15mm/0.59in
**Powerplant:** V-59 12-cylinder 382kW/520hp
　　multi-fuel diesel engine
**Performance:** Speed – 63kph/39mph
　　Range – 500km/311 miles

# 2S19 152mm Self-Propelled Gun

In 1985 work started on a replacement weapon for the 2S3 and the 2S5 self-propelled guns. The new vehicle would use parts from both the T-72 and T-80 tanks, and a new gun was to be developed as the 2A33 had been in use since 1955. The 2S19 was accepted for service with the Soviet Army in 1989 and given the name of Msta-S. This was a departure from the previous practice of naming SPGs after flowers or plants as the Msta was a river in the Ilmen district of Russia.

The 2S19 uses the hull and suspension of the T-80 tank, but the tried and tested 12-cylinder diesel engine of the T-72. The first, second and sixth road wheels are equipped with regulated telescopic shock absorbers which are controlled when firing the gun so the vehicle does not require a recoil spade on the rear. The driver's compartment is the same as that in the T-80 and has no connection with the crew in the turret except by internal intercom. The turret sits on the top of the chassis and can traverse through 360 degrees. It is equipped with two loading systems: a fully automatic loader for the warheads, and a semi-automatic loader for the propulsion charges. These two systems allow the 2S19 to maintain a high rate of sustained accurate fire and it can hit 38 out of 40 targets at a range of 15km/9.3 miles. The auto-loaders can reload the gun at any angle so the gun does not have to return to the horizontal position

between rounds. The turret has an independent power supply from the main vehicle and this allows the diesel engine to be switched off during combat to suppress its heat signature. This is essential on the modern battlefield as the latest guided weapons can be targeted on to a heat source such as a hot engine or exhaust vents.

Like most Soviet weaponry, this vehicle is widely exported. In 2000, the basic export version of the 2S19 cost 1.6 million US dollars, and a special export version that will fire standard NATO ammunition has also been developed.

TOP: **This vehicle has an extremely long barrel, which shows up well in this picture. The very robust travel lock can be seen at the rear end of the barrel. On the front of the turret are six smoke dischargers and the vehicle commander's cupola has been fitted with a machine-gun.**

ABOVE: **The very large turret covers the top of the T-80 tank hull and chassis. On the end of the barrel is a double-baffle muzzle brake.**

LEFT: **A rear view of the 2S19. Under the rear of the turret are the engine grills. On the back of the turret is a large conveyor, which is used for resupplying ammunition into the turret. Towards the front of the turret on each side are large access hatches for the crew.**

## 2S19 152mm SPG

**Country:** USSR
**Entered service:** 1989
**Crew:** 5 plus 2 extra loaders
**Weight:** 41,961kg/41.3 tons
**Dimensions:** Length – 11.92m/39ft 1in
　　Height – 2.99m/9ft 10in
　　Width – 3.38m/11ft 1in
**Armament:** Main – 2A64 152mm/5.98in howitzer
　　Secondary – 12.7mm/0.5in NSVT machine-gun
**Armour:** Classified
**Powerplant:** V-84A 12-cylinder 626kW/840hp multi-fuel diesel engine
**Performance:** Speed – 60kph/37mph
　　Range – 500km/311 miles

LEFT: This Abbot is on a live-firing exercise. The additional ammunition supply has been dropped at the rear of the vehicle; the rounds are delivered in plastic cases. The large rear door is used for passing ammunition through to the gun crew. The small hatch above the main door is for communication.
ABOVE: The compact size of the Abbot can be clearly seen. The chassis is the same as the FV 432 armoured personnel carrier. Running along the side of the vehicle above the track is the exhaust system for the vehicle.

# Abbot 105mm Self-Propelled Gun

In the late 1950s NATO decided that the 105mm/4.13in calibre would be adopted as the standard close-support shell size. As a result, Britain had to retire the 25pdr gun and design a new weapon. The first Abbot prototype was produced in 1961, with the first vehicle being issued for service in 1965. It would remain in service until replaced by the AS90 in 1995.

The main production line was located at the Vickers Armstrong works in

LEFT: The barrel of this Abbot is at maximum elevation. On the front of the turret are two clusters of smoke dischargers. There is a bank of four headlights on the hull front. The travel lock for the gun barrel is in the upright position.

Newcastle-upon-Tyne. The Abbot was the field artillery version of the FV 432 family but the Abbot only used the engine and suspension of the FV 432. The vehicle was an all-welded construction. The driver was located on the right at the front of the vehicle with the engine next to him on the left. Mounted at the rear of the vehicle was a large spacious turret, which housed the three remaining members of the crew and had storage for 40 rounds of ammunition although only 38 were normally carried. The turret had a power-operated traverse but gun-elevation was performed by hand. A power rammer was installed to aid ramming the shells into the gun and a semi-automatic vertical sliding breach was also fitted. The gun had a maximum range of 17,000m/55,775ft and a maximum rate of fire of 12 rounds per minute, but this could not be sustained for long. Access to the fighting compartment was via a single large door in the rear of the vehicle and this was also used to pass

ammunition to the gun when tasked with a sustained fire mission. Six of the rounds carried in the turret were HESH (High-Explosive Squash-Head); this was an anti-tank round that was provided for use in the event of an engagement with enemy tanks. The Abbot was permanently fitted with a flotation screen to allow river-crossing and could be erected by the crew in 15 minutes.

Vickers also produced a simplified version for export but the only customer was India. An Abbot regiment consisted of three batteries, each with two troops of three guns supported in the field by the Stalwart 6x6 high-mobility load carrier.

## Abbot 105mm SPG

**Country:** UK
**Entered service:** 1965
**Crew:** 4
**Weight:** 17,475kg/17.2 tons
**Dimensions:** Length – 5.84m/19ft 2in
    Height – 2.48m/8ft 2in
    Width – 2.64m/8ft 8in
**Armament:** Main – 105mm/4.13in L13A1 gun
    Secondary – 7.62mm/0.3in L4A4 machine-gun
**Armour:** Maximum – 12mm/0.47in
**Powerplant:** Rolls-Royce K60 6-cylinder
    179kW/240hp multi-fuel diesel engine
**Performance:** Speed – 50kph/30mph
    Range – 395km/245 miles

# AMX-10P Mechanized Infantry Combat Vehicle

The AMX (*Atelier de Construction d'Issy les Moulineaux*) company started development on this vehicle in 1965 to meet a requirement from the French Army for a replacement for the AMX VCI infantry vehicle. The first prototype was finished in 1968 and proved to be unacceptable to the army, so major changes were made to the design, and new prototypes were produced. The resulting new vehicle was higher, wider and had a two-man 20mm/0.79in turret. The trials were completed successfully and the revised vehicle entered service with the French Army in 1973 as the AMX-10P.

The hull of the vehicle is made of all-welded construction with the driver's compartment at the front of the vehicle on the left-hand side. To the right of the driver is the main engine compartment which houses the Hispano-Suiza super-charged diesel engine. The engine compartment is fitted with aircraft engine-style fire-extinguishing equipment and the engine pack can be changed in just two hours. The AMX-10P is fully amphibious and has two water jets fitted to the rear of the vehicle to propel it when in the water. The two-man Toucan II turret is mounted in the centre of the vehicle, offset slightly to the left. The 20mm/0.79in cannon is mounted on the outside of the turret and has a dual-feed ammunition system which allows the gunner to select either HE (High-Explosive) or AP (Armour-Piercing)

ammunition. The turret carries 325 rounds which are made up of 260 rounds HE in one belt and 65 AP rounds in the other and the gunner can switch between belts while firing. The infantry compartment in the rear of the vehicle has accommodation for eight men, and is accessed via an electrically operated ramp at the back.

The basic AMX-10P has been developed into a complete family of vehicles numbering some 15 different types. A close-support version known as "Marine" has been produced for amphibious operations and is armed with a 90mm/3.54in gun.

The French Army has taken delivery of 2,500 of the AMX-10P, while the largest export order was for 300 vehicles for Saudi Arabia. Production of this vehicle has now finished.

TOP: **The 20mm/0.79in turret is mounted in the middle of the vehicle, while around the front of the turret is a bank of smoke dischargers. Down the side of this vehicle is a series of equipment attachment points.** ABOVE: **The large hydraulic ramp can clearly be seen. The men leaving the vehicle are carrying AT missiles. On each corner at the rear of the vehicle are two twin smoke dischargers. This vehicle is fitted with a MILAN AT system.**

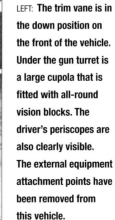

LEFT: **The trim vane is in the down position on the front of the vehicle. Under the gun turret is a large cupola that is fitted with all-round vision blocks. The driver's periscopes are also clearly visible. The external equipment attachment points have been removed from this vehicle.**

## AMX-10P MICV

**Country:** France
**Entered service:** 1973
**Crew:** 3 plus 8 infantry
**Weight:** 13,818kg/13.6 tons
**Dimensions:** Length – 5.82m/18ft 1in
    Height – 2.54m/8ft 4in
    Width – 2.78m/9ft 2in
**Armament:** Main 1 x 20mm/0.79in M693 cannon,
    and 1 x coaxial 7.62mm/0.3in machine-gun
    Secondary – Small arms
**Armour:** Classified
**Powerplant:** Hispano-Suiza HS-115 8-cylinder
    194kW/260hp super-charged diesel engine
**Performance:** Speed – 65kph/40mph
    Range – 600km/370 miles

# AMX-10RC Armoured Car

ABOVE: **The boat-shaped hull of the AMX-10RC can be clearly seen in this picture. The gun barrel of this vehicle has a very long overhang. The wheels are in the raised position.**

Development on the AMX-10RC started in September 1970 to meet a French Army requirement for a replacement for the Panhard EBR heavy armoured car. The first three prototypes were built in June 1971 and then a six-year trials and development period started which ended when the car was accepted for service in 1977. The AMX-10RC entered service in 1978 and by the time the production run was finished in 1987, the French Army had taken delivery of 207 cars, while the largest export contract (for 108 vehicles) was to Morocco, North Africa.

The all-welded aluminium hull and turret provide bullet and shell-splinter protection for the crew. The driver is positioned in the front of the vehicle on the left-hand side, with the main fighting compartment in the middle and the turret on the top. The engine is in the rear of the vehicle and is the same as that fitted to the AMX-10P MICV. The gearbox has two functions: one is to drive the vehicle in both directions using a pre-selection through four gears in both directions, and the other is to supply power to the two water-jets that are mounted on the rear of the car to propel it through the water. None of the wheels on the vehicle turns as the car uses the same skid-steering system as a tracked vehicle. The suspension is hydro-pneumatic and allows the vehicle to change its ride height depending on the terrain encountered. The vehicle is fitted with a full NBC system and night-fighting optics.

The AMX-10RC has a three-man turret with the commander and gunner on the right and the loader/radio operator on the left. The COTAC fire-control system is composed of a number of sensors that provide the computer with the following data: target range, speed, angle of cant and wind speed, while altitude and outside temperature are fed into the computer by the gunner. A laser is used for measuring the distance to the target and is effective from 400–10,000m/1,312–32,808ft. The vehicle commander can override the gunner and take over the aiming of the gun. This vehicle is currently in service with France and two other countries.

## AMX-10RC Armoured Car

**Country:** France
**Entered service:** 1978
**Crew:** 4
**Weight:** 15,850kg/15.6 tons
**Dimensions:** Length – 9.15m/30ft
    Height – 2.69m/8ft 10in
    Width – 2.95m/9ft 8in
**Armament:** Main – 1 x 105mm/4.13in gun, and
    1 x 7.62mm/0.3in coaxial machine-gun
    Secondary – None
**Armour:** classified
**Powerplant:** Hispano-Suiza HS-115 8-cylinder
    194kW/260hp supercharged diesel engine
**Performance:** Speed – Road 85kph/53mph;
    Water 7.2kph/4.5mph
    Range – 1,000km/621 miles

ABOVE: **The grill behind the rear wheel is the intake for the water-jet propulsion system. The trim vane is folded down on the top of the glacis plate.**

# AMX-13 DCA SPAAG

The first prototypes of the AMX DCA were completed in 1960, but were not fitted with the guidance radar as it was not yet ready. The first radar-equipped prototype was built in 1964 and was tested by the French Army until 1966, when an order was placed for 60 vehicles that were to be delivered and in service by 1969.

The AMX DCA system was mounted on the AMX-13 light tank chassis in a very similar way to that of the 105mm/4.13in SPG vehicle conversion. The driver was seated in the front of the vehicle on the left with the engine next to him on the right. The SAMM turret with positions for the other two members of the crew was mounted on the rear of the vehicle. The vehicle commander sat on the left with the gunner on the right, and between them were the twin 30mm/1.18in cannon, while mounted on the top rear of the turret was a pulse-Doppler DR-VC-1A radar dish. When the vehicle was moving, this was stowed in a lightly armoured box. Both the commander and gunner could traverse the turret. Each gun could be selected either independently of the other or both together while the gunner could select single-shot, bursts of 5 or 15 rounds or fully automatic fire. The turret carried 600 rounds of belt-fed ammunition, 300 rounds per gun. The rate of fire of the guns per barrel was 600 rounds per minute, which gave the turret a 30-second supply of ammunition. The maximum range of the guns was 3,000m/9,842ft and all the empty cartridges and links were ejected to the outside of the turret. The turret also carried all the optical, electrical and hydraulic systems for the guns.

In the late 1960s the French took the DCA turret and mounted it on the AMX-30 tank chassis, but the improvement in mobility did not impress the French Army and so the project was dropped. In 1975, Saudi Arabia asked for the system but with an improved ammunition supply to 1,200 rounds, and subsequently placed an order for 56 vehicles.

ABOVE: **This is an early version of the AMX-13 DCA. The vehicle uses the chassis of the AMX-13 light tank. The guns are at 45 degrees of elevation. Two further 300-round belts of ammunition are carried below the turret in the body of the vehicle.**

ABOVE: **The vents for the exhaust system can be seen running down the side of the vehicle. On each side of the turret is a pair of smoke dischargers. The turret crew have remote gun-control boxes in front of them.** LEFT: **This is one of the prototype vehicles as it has no fittings on the turret. The three crew positions can be clearly seen on this vehicle.**

## AMX-13 DCA SPAAG

**Country:** France
**Entered service:** 1968
**Crew:** 3
**Weight:** 15,037kg/14.8 tons
**Dimensions:** Length – 5.4m/17ft 9in
Height – 3.8m/12ft 6in (radar operating)
Width – 2.5m/8ft 2in
**Armament:** Main – 2 x 30mm/1.18in HSS-831A
automatic cannon
Secondary – None
**Armour:** Maximum – 30mm/1.18in
**Powerplant:** SOFAM 8-cylinder 201kW/270hp
petrol engine
**Performance:** Speed – 60kph/37mph
Range – 350km/215 miles

LEFT: **The extremely long gun barrel of this SPG is clearly visible. The GCT does not require any outriggers to stabilize the vehicle when firing due to the hydraulic shock absorbers. The extra long recuperators can be seen mounted under and over the gun barrel.**

# AMX GCT 155mm Self-Propelled Gun

In the late 1960s, the French Army required a replacement for the ageing 105mm/4.13in Mk 61 and the 155mm/6.1in Mk F3 self-propelled guns, both of which used the AMX-13 light tank chassis. Development of the new vehicle started in 1969. The first prototype was completed in 1972 and went on public display the next year. Between 1974 and 1975 ten vehicles were built for trials with the French Army. The AMX GCT (*Grande Cadence de Tir*) finally entered production in 1977, with the first vehicles being sold to Saudi Arabia. It was accepted for service in the French Army in July 1979.

The chassis used was the AMX-30 MBT (Main Battle Tank). The engine and suspension were untouched in this conversion; the main area affected being the turret. This was removed together with all the ammunition storage in the body of the tank and was replaced by a generator and ventilator, which fed fresh air to the new 155mm/6.1in gun turret. The driver sits in the front of the vehicle on the left-hand side and has three periscopes in front of him, the central one of which can be

replaced by an infrared or image-intensifier periscope for night driving. The engine is at the rear of the vehicle and is a Hispano-Suiza HS 110 supercharged multi-fuel unit. The complete engine pack can be removed by a three-man team in as little as 45 minutes. The gearbox is mechanically operated and has just five gears for both forward and reverse, and is combined with the steering mechanism. The suspension system uses torsion bars and the first and last road wheels are fitted with hydraulic shock absorbers.

The turret is of all-welded construction with the commander and gunner stationed on the right of the turret and the loader on the left. The commander's cupola is fixed but has periscopes mounted all around it to give 360 degrees of sight. The loader has a hatch as he operates the anti-aircraft machine-gun that can be either a 7.62mm/0.3in or 12.7mm/0.5in weapon. The gun crew enter the turret through two side doors, the door on the left opening towards the front while the door on the right opens towards the rear. The turret and the breech are hydraulically operated. The breech is a vertically sliding wedge breech block which is hermetically sealed by a blanking plate. There are manual controls for use in the event of the vehicle losing hydraulic power. The gun takes just two minutes to bring into action and, in case of counter-battery fire, just one minute to take out of action and start to move the vehicle. The average rate of fire using the automatic loader is eight rounds per minute, while with manual loading the rate of fire falls to just three rounds per minute. The gun is capable of firing six rounds in just 45 seconds in what is called "burst firing". The ammunition is stored in the rear of the turret in two separate sections; in one box are

LEFT: **A night-firing exercise. The sheer size of the turret can be seen when compared to the hull of the AMX-30. This gives the vehicle a high centre of gravity.**

42 projectiles and in the other are 42 cartridge cases with propellant. A further 40 propellant charges can be stored in a fixed container under the turret. The turret is resupplied with ammunition through two large doors in the rear which fold down and form a platform for the reloading crew. The gun can be reloaded while still firing and a full reload will take a crew of four men 15 minutes or two men 20 minutes. The normal maximum range of the gun is 18,000m/59,055ft, but using rocket-assisted ammunition, this can be increased to 30,500m/100,065ft. Both the vehicle and the turret are fitted with a full NBC system and there is no recoil spade attached to the rear.

The turret can be adapted to fit many different MBT chassis including the German Leopard and the Russian T-72 and it is in service with three other countries in addition to France. In 2005, the French upgraded the engine to the Renault E9 diesel. The French Army have 190 AMX GCTs in service and so far, an additional 400 of these vehicles have been built for foreign customers.

ABOVE LEFT: **This GCT turret has been fitted to the T-72 hull and chassis. This is an Egyptian vehicle. The turret has also been developed to fit the German Leopard hull and chassis.** ABOVE: **The gun is at maximum elevation. The barrel is fitted with a large double-baffle muzzle brake. The lower front of the turret has two clusters of three smoke dischargers fitted.**

ABOVE: **A GCT on exercise. This vehicle has been fitted with a 12.7mm/0.5in heavy machine-gun on the top of the turret.**
RIGHT: **The rear of the turret opens downward and exposes the ammunition racks. The gun can continue to fire even with the back down. Full reloading takes the crew of the vehicle just 15 minutes.**

## AMX 155mm GCT SPG

**Country:** France
**Entered service:** 1980
**Crew:** 4
**Weight:** 41,961kg/41.3 tons
**Dimensions:** Length – 10.4m/34ft 1in
    Height – 3.25m/10ft 8in
    Width – 3.15m/10ft 4in
**Armament:** Main – 155mm/6.1in howitzer
    Secondary – 1 x 7.62mm/0.3in or 1 x 12.7mm/
    0.5in machine-gun
**Armour:** Maximum – 30mm/1.18in (estimated)
**Powerplant:** Hispano-Suiza HS 110 537kW/720hp
    multi-fuel engine
**Performance:** Speed – 60kph/37mph
    Range – 450km/280 miles

# AMX VCI Infantry Combat Vehicle

The AMX VCI (*Véhicule de Combat d'Infanterie*) was developed in the early 1950s to meet a requirement for the French Army following the cancellation of the Hotchkiss TT6 and TT9 APCs. The first prototype was completed in 1955 with production starting in 1957.

The AMX VCI used the chassis and the front of the hull up to and including the driver's compartment of the AMX-13 tank. The hull behind the driver was increased in height to allow for troops to be seated in the rear of the vehicle. The infantry compartment in the rear held ten men seated back to back, five on each side. There were four firing ports in the side and two in the rear doors, which opened outwards. The vehicle had no NBC equipment at first but this was later fitted as an upgrade to all vehicles. The driver was in the front of the vehicle on the left, with the engine compartment on the right. Behind and above the driver was the vehicle gunner and the vehicle commander was next to him. When this vehicle originally came into service the gunner used a 7.5mm/0.295in machine-gun. This was quickly improved to a

12.7mm/0.5in heavy machine-gun, which was subsequently modified to a CAFL 38 turret armed with a 7.62mm/0.3in machine-gun which could be aimed and fired from inside the vehicle. The French then went on to develop a number of turrets that could be fitted to the vehicle ranging from a twin 7.62mm/0.3in Creusot-Loire TLiG to a CB20 20mm/0.79in turret. The AMX VCI was not amphibious but could ford shallow water and a splash board was

ABOVE: **The hatches above the rear crew area are in the open position. The turret gunner is in his turret, with the vehicle commander next to him. The compact size of the vehicle can be seen clearly in this picture.**

mounted on the glacis plate at the front of the vehicle to facilitate this.

The AMX VCI was developed into a family of vehicles with ten different variations. In total 15,000 of this family of vehicles were built of which 3,000 were the VCI version, and they are still in service with ten different countries. It was replaced in French service by the AMX-10P from 1977. The rest of the AMX family were phased out by 1982.

RIGHT: **The small square hatches in the top rear of the crew compartment are the firing ports. The dome under the turret is part of the air filter system.**

LEFT: **The turret of the AMX is armed with a single 12.7mm/0.5in machine-gun. The large driver's visor can be seen on the left of the vehicle. The gap between the tracks has been closed by a splash plate. The headlights are mounted halfway up the glacis plate.**

## AMX VCI Infantry Combat Vehicle

**Country:** France
**Entered service:** 1958
**Crew:** 3 plus 10 infantry
**Weight:** 14,021kg/13.8 tons
**Dimensions:** Length – 5.54m/18ft 2in
    Height – 2.32m/7ft 7in
    Width – 2.51m/8ft 3in
**Armament:** Main 1 x 12.7mm/0.5in machine-gun
    or 1 x 7.62mm/0.3in machine-gun, basic fit
    Secondary – Small arms
**Armour:** Maximum – 30mm/1.18in
**Powerplant:** SOFAM 8 GXB, 8-cylinder
    186kW/250hp petrol engine
**Performance:** Speed – 65kph/40mph
    Range – 400km/250 miles

# Modern Armoured Fighting Vehicle

## Comments on articles, read at random

p.72    Honest John! Most of article and data table is for the M31 version w/ long launcher
     but the 3 photos are of the short launcher fr- the M50 version. whole article confusing!

p.15    BTR-60 labeled as BTR-70 in photo.        MICV not defined

p.9    TEL not defined.

19    AIFV not defined    ? Armored Infantry F.V.

28-29    The position of engine differs in the text and the drawings.   text! engine alongside driver   dwg! " behind "

36    bottom phot! cannot see the grill described in the photo.

LEFT: This is the six-wheeled Fuchs NBC vehicle. The commander's door is open, and a machine-gun has been mounted above his position. The rear of the vehicle is covered in personal kit. BELOW: This is the 4x4 version of the Fuchs. The exhaust system can be seen on the hull side; it exits the vehicle under the main armament and runs back along the length of the vehicle. This Fuchs is armed with a single 2cm/0.79in cannon.

# APC Transportpanzer 1 Fuchs

The development of this vehicle dates back to 1964, when the German Army were looking for a family of vehicles that would be capable of covering most of their future non-tank AFV requirements. This new generation of vehicles was to be developed using three new chassis, a 4x4, a 6x6 and an 8x8, for tactical trucks, reconnaissance vehicles and APCs. MAN won the contract to deliver the new trucks and Rheinmetall won the contract to supply the 6x6 armoured amphibious load carriers that became the Transportpanzer 1.

The Transportpanzer 1 is an all-welded steel construction and protects the crew from bullets and shell-splinters. The hull also has spaced armour in a number of critical places. The driver sits on the left in the front of the vehicle with the commander next to him on the right. Both the driver and the commander have their own access doors in the front of the vehicle and both doors have large windows that can be covered by an armoured shutter. The vehicle has a large single windscreen for both the driver and commander and gives an excellent field of vision. This is a bullet-proof screen but can be covered by an armoured shutter that folds down from the top of the vehicle. The engine compartment is behind the driver on the left of the vehicle with a small passageway linking the front to the rear crew compartment. The engine compartment is fitted with an automatic fire-extinguishing system and the complete engine pack can be removed in just ten minutes. The troop cargo area in the rear holds ten men in two rows of five sitting facing each other. The vehicle is fitted with a full NBC system and night-driving equipment.

The German Army started to take delivery of their vehicles in 1979 with the last batch being delivered in 1986; in total 996 were supplied. Britain, Holland and the USA have all bought a special contamination-measuring version that is fitted for NBC and electronic warfare. The vehicle is still in service with a number of armies around the world.

LEFT: The four-wheel steering can be clearly seen on this vehicle. The large trim vane is folded back on the front of the vehicle. The armoured shutter above the screen is half deployed.

## APC Transportpanzer 1 Fuchs

**Country:** Germany
**Entered service:** 1979
**Crew:** 2 plus 10 infantry
**Weight:** 16,967kg/16.7 tons
**Dimensions:** Length – 6.83m/22ft 5in
  Height – 2.3m/7ft 7in
  Width – 2.98m/9ft 9in
**Armament:** Main – None
  Secondary – None
**Armour:** Classified
**Powerplant:** Mercedes-Benz V8 8-cylinder
  239kW/320hp diesel engine
**Performance:** Speed – 105kph/65mph
  Range – 800km/500 miles

# AS90 155mm Self-Propelled Gun

In the late 1960s, the British Army started to look for a replacement for the 105mm/4.13in Abbot and the American 155mm/6.1in M109. It was to be built by a consortium of firms from three countries: Britain, Germany and Italy. Britain was to produce the turret and sights, Germany would produce the engine, the hull and the main gun, and Italy would produce the recoil, fuel and loading systems. This new weapon system was due to go into service in 1980 but the project disintegrated with each of the participating countries going their own way, resulting in the joint venture being finally wound up in 1986. Vickers, the British firm in the consortium, decided to go it alone and produce a private venture vehicle using the FH70 gun that they had developed along with the German and Italian companies. The new vehicle they built was designated the GBT 155 and this

ABOVE: **The soldier at the rear of the vehicle is standing under the auxiliary power unit which is fitted to the rear of the turret. A wire-mesh storage box has been fitted to the top of the turret for the storage of camouflage netting and tents.** BELOW LEFT: **The vehicle commander in his cupola is giving directions to the driver. The hatch in the side of the turret is folded back to give increased ventilation to the turret.** BELOW: **The gun barrel is locked into the travel lock, which when not in use folds back on to the glacis plate. On the front of the turret is one of the two clusters of smoke dischargers.**

would become the prototype for the AS90. It was ready for testing in 1982, while the second prototype was ready to join the test programme in 1986. This new vehicle entered the competition for the replacement for the Abbot in 1989 and won, with the result that the army placed a fixed-price contract of

300 million pounds for 179 AS90 units. The first AS90 vehicles entered service in 1993 with the final deliveries to the British Army being made in 1995, replacing all its other self-propelled guns.

The AS90 uses a specially developed turret and chassis, but is otherwise constructed using a large number of standard parts from other vehicles in service with the British Army. It is of all-welded steel construction, which is bullet and shell-splinter proof. The driver sits in the front of the vehicle on the left-hand side, while alongside is the main power pack, consisting of a Cummins diesel engine. The turret houses the other four men in the crew, with the gunner and the vehicle commander, stationed on the right and the shell loader and the charge loader, on the left. Above the loaders is a hatch with an anti-aircraft 7.62mm/0.3in or 12.7mm/0.5in pintle-mounted machine-gun. The commander has a cupola with all-round vision. The turret houses all the targeting computers, direct sights and fully automatic gun-laying equipment, and also has an ammunition management system and a fully automatic loading system. Thirty-one warheads are stored in the turret bustle, with a further seventeen stored under the turret, which has a full 360-degree traverse. The normal maximum range of the FH70 155mm/6.1in 39-calibre gun is 24,700m/81,036ft but by using rocket-assisted ammunition the range can be extended to 30,000m/98,425ft. The gun can elevate to maximum of 70 degrees, and has a minimum range of 2,500m/8,200ft. It can fire three rounds in less than 10 seconds and has a sustained rate of fire of two rounds per minute. The suspension is hydro-pneumatic which not only gives the vehicle excellent cross-country ability but also ensures a comfortable ride for the crew.

In 2005 the AS90 underwent an upgrade as it was quickly decided that the armour was too thin, the range of the gun needed increasing, and laser targeting was required. The upgrades have resulted in the vehicle now known as the AS90 Braveheart. The armour is fully bullet-proof and can even withstand a 14.55mm/0.57in anti-tank round. The roof of the turret has been fitted with a thermal shield to protect the crew from heat in desert conditions. BAE Systems have been awarded the contract to upgrade 96 of the basic AS90s to the new Braveheart standard. This also includes a new, longer 52-calibre gun barrel which increases the basic range of the gun to 40,000m/131,240ft. The new upgraded vehicles were due to be finished and back in service by 2003, but this was halted while further testing was being carried out. However, the new enhanced SPGs are expected to be in service by 2007. Poland has placed an order for 72 new AS90 vehicles to replace their ageing Soviet 2S3 self-propelled guns.

ABOVE: This AS90 has had a machine-gun fitted to the commander's position. Behind the fume extractor on the barrel of the gun is a rubber protective sleeve which helps keep dirt from entering the turret. BELOW: The crew of this AS90 are about to break camp. The vehicle would be placed in this type of hide each time it is stationary for long periods of time. Vehicles on the modern battlefield have to hide to survive.

ABOVE: The large storage boxes on the side of the turret can be clearly seen, along with the empty wire-mesh bin on the roof of the vehicle. The large door in the rear of the vehicle is in the open position; this is the main entrance and exit from the vehicle. The AS90 turret has also been fitted to the Indian T-72 MBT chassis for trials with the Indian Army.

## AS90 155mm SPG

**Country:** UK
**Entered service:** 1993
**Crew:** 5
**Weight:** 45,000kg/44.3 tons
**Dimensions:** Length – 9.9m/32ft 6in
　　Height – 3m/9ft 10in
　　Width – 3.4m/11ft 4in
**Armament:** Main – FH70 155mm/6.1in howitzer
　　Secondary – 7.62mm/0.3in machine-gun
**Armour:** Maximum – 17mm/0.67in
**Powerplant:** Cummins VTA 903T 660T-660
　　8-cylinder 492kW/660hp diesel engine
**Performance:** Speed – 55kph/34mph
　　Range – 370km/230 miles

LEFT: **This BMD is taking part in a November Parade in Moscow in 1981. The top of the commander's hatch has the badge of the Soviet Airborne Forces painted on it. The six men of the infantry section carried in the vehicle can be seen sitting on the rear of the BMD.** BELOW: **A side view of a BMD during a parade in Moscow. A Sagger AT missile is in place on its launcher on the top of the gun barrel.**

# BMD Airborne Combat Vehicles

When the Soviet Union was forced into a humiliating climb down after the Cuban Missile Crisis in 1963, it was decided to expand and upgrade the Soviet Airborne Forces (VDV). It was very quickly realized that the paratroopers required some form of mechanization to combat anti-personnel weapons and to give them better mobility once on the ground. Development started on the BMD in about 1965. The first production vehicles were issued for service in 1969, and it was first seen by the West in 1970.

The BMD is the only airborne infantry vehicle in service anywhere in the world and it was initially thought by NATO to be an airborne tank. The driver/mechanic is seated in the centre-front of the vehicle with the gun barrel just above his head, while the vehicle commander and radio operator is to the left and slightly to the rear. To the right of the driver is the bow machine-gunner, and behind them is the turret with a single gunner in it. This is the same turret as fitted to the BMP and can fire Sagger wire-guided anti-tank missiles. Behind this is an infantry compartment that was originally designed to accommodate six men, but this has been reduced to five as the vehicle is very small and cramped for the crew. The vehicle is fully amphibious and has two water jets mounted on the rear for propulsion. A protective splash board is fitted on the glacis plate and this is raised when the vehicle enters the water. The turret is fitted with a low-pressure 73mm/2.87in gun fed by a 40-round magazine. The gun fires fin-stabilized HEAT (High-Explosive Anti-Tank) or HE-FRAG (High-Explosive Fragmentation) rounds. Once the round leaves the barrel,

a rocket motor fires in its rear and increases the speed of the round and its range to 1,300m/4,265ft, but this system is adversely affected by the weather and wind, reducing its accuracy greatly.

The Soviet Army realized that the three cargo parachutes that were required to drop the vehicle safely from an aircraft were very heavy, but that they could reduce this to a single parachute by fitting rockets to the PRSM-915 pallet used for air-launching the vehicle. As the pallet leaves the aircraft, four wires with ground contact sensors fitted to their ends are released under the pallet. When one of these sensors strikes the ground, the rockets are fired and these slow the vehicle down for a safe landing. They also realized that dropping the vehicle without its driver and gunner made it very vulnerable,

LEFT: **This vehicle is the improved BMD-2. It is armed with a 30mm/1.18in cannon in the turret. The chassis has five road wheels, with the drive wheel at the rear of the vehicle. The air intake for the engine can be seen in the middle of the glacis.** BELOW: **These two BMDs are on exercise. When the driver is in his raised driving position then the gun barrel has to be at maximum elevation.**

so at first the driver and gunner descended in the vehicle. The idea was that they could very quickly dispose of the parachutes, drive the vehicle off the pallet and go to find the rest of the crew. The vehicle would be dropped from a maximum height of 457.2m/1,500ft and the descent takes less than one minute. A great deal of courage was required by the crew to be in the vehicle when it leaves the aircraft especially as a number of accidents occurred in the development of this system, killing the crew. A new system has subsequently been developed where radio beacons are fitted to each vehicle, each one having a different signal, so that the crew can drop separately yet find their vehicle very quickly and move off into action.

Development of the BMD-2 was started in 1983 as an interim solution to combat reports from Afghanistan that showed a number of faults with the BMDs, which were the first vehicles into the country. In particular the 73mm/2.87in gun was shown to be very poor and so the turret was replaced in the BMD-2 with a new one armed with a 30mm/1.18in cannon.

Production started in 1985 and it entered service the same year. The BMD-3 was developed to overcome problems with the track and suspension, and the engine was also upgraded to a more powerful diesel. This new vehicle was due to go into service by 1990 but this was delayed by a year. Due to money problems in Russia this programme is still continuing, but very slowly. Russia is the only country to develop this kind of vehicle. Several specialist vehicles of the BMD-3 are under development at this time and the 125mm/4.92in 2S25 SPATG uses many of the components of the BMD-3.

RIGHT: **This BMD-2 is taking part in an informal parade. The turret has an infrared light fitted to the side. At the rear of the turret is a pintle mount for a Spigot or Spandrel AT missile. This is the same turret as mounted on the BMP-2.**

### BMD-1 Airborne Combat Vehicle

**Country:** USSR
**Entered service:** 1969
**Crew:** 2 plus 5 infantry
**Weight:** 6,807kg/6.7 tons
**Dimensions:** Length – 5.4m/17ft 9in
　　Height – 1.77m/5ft 10in
　　Width –2.55m/8ft 4in
**Armament:** Main – 1 x 2A28 73mm/2.87in gun,
　　and 1 x coaxial 7.62mm/0.3in machine-gun
　　Secondary – 2 x 7.62mm/0.3in machine-guns,
　　and 1 x Sagger launch rail
**Armour:** Maximum – 23mm/0.91in
**Powerplant:** 5D20 6-cylinder 216kW/290hp
　　diesel engine
**Performance:** Speed – Road 80kph/50mph;
　　Water 10kph/6mph
　　Range – 320km/199 miles

LEFT: **The low profile of the BMP-1 turret can be clearly seen. The chassis is made up of six road wheels with the driving wheel at the front. The upper part of the track is covered by a skirt.** ABOVE: **A BMP-1 leaving the water, with the trim vane in the raised position. The crew are in the closed-down position. The transition to amphibious vehicle only takes a few minutes.**

# BMP-1 Infantry Fighting Vehicle

The BMP (*Boevaya Mashina Pekhota*) was the world's first infantry combat vehicle and was the most significant innovation in infantry combat tactics of the late 20th century. It was also the first Soviet military vehicle to be designed with the needs of the nuclear battlefield in mind. This new vehicle provided the infantry with unprecedented firepower, mobility and protection that could be taken into the heart of the enemy position and the idea would be copied in vehicles such as the American Bradley, the German Marder and the British Warrior.

Development started in the 1960s and prototypes were ready for testing in 1964. In 1966 the BMP-1 was accepted for service and placed into production, but, due to a number of problems that subsequently came to light, mass production was not started until 1970. The BMP-1 is of an all-welded steel construction which offers protection from bullets and shell-splinters; the front is even proof against 12.7mm/0.5in anti-tank rounds. The glacis plate is distinctively ribbed with the driver located behind the ribbed area on the left-hand side of the vehicle and the commander seated behind. The engine is mounted on the right-hand side of the vehicle next to the driver and commander while the air intakes and outlets are on the top of the vehicle. Two forms of starting the main engine are fitted; either compressed air or battery. The compressed air system is normally used in very cold winter temperatures.

Behind the commander and the engine is a one-man turret which is equipped with the 73mm/2.87in smooth-bore low-pressure gun, fed from a 40-round magazine. On leaving the barrel, a rocket motor in the tail of each round is ignited, but these munitions are badly affected by the wind and the weather. The maximum rate of fire is eight rounds per minute.

RIGHT: **The driver of this BMP-1 is standing in front of his vehicle in Afghanistan. The vehicle has been fitted with additional storage on the rear of the turret. The three pistol ports are open on the rear. The ribbed glacis plate can be clearly seen here. A large searchlight has been fitted in front of the commander's hatch but behind the driver's position.**

Mounted coaxially to the main gun is a 7.62mm/0.3in PKT machine-gun which is fed by a 2,000-round belt housed in a box under the turret, while mounted over the main armament is a rail for a Sagger wire-guided anti-tank missile. The Sagger has a minimum range of 500m/1,640ft and a maximum of 3,000m/9,842ft. One missile is carried on the rail in the ready-to-use position, while two others are stored in the turret. Reloading takes 50 seconds. The missile controls are stored under the gunner's seat and these are pulled out and locked in position between his legs when required. After firing, the gunner watches the missile through a scope while controlling its flight using a joystick. This missile system can only be used in daylight as there is no other way of tracking it.

The BMP-1 has a full NBC air-filtration system. The troop compartment in the rear holds eight men, four down each side sitting back to back facing the outside of the vehicle. The main fuel tank is positioned between the backs of these men, while the rear doors of the vehicle are also fuel tanks, giving a total fuel capacity of 460 litres/101 gallons. This fuel storage system poses considerable risks to both vehicle and occupants on the battlefield. In the roof of the troop compartment are four hatches for the infantry to use and each man also has a firing port in front of his position in the rear of the vehicle. Apart from the men's own personal weapons an RPG-7 anti-tank grenade launcher is also carried. It has been found that the vehicle is very cramped under service conditions due to the low height of the roof and several countries using the BMP-1 have reduced the number of troops in the infantry section in the rear to six men. The vehicle also has a very poor ventilation system so the rear compartment becomes unbearably hot.

The BMP-1 is fully amphibious and is propelled through the water by the vehicle's own tracks. Just before entering the water, a trim vane is attached to the front of the vehicle, the bilge pumps are switched on and the splash plate is raised. When in the water the BMP-1 is driven in third gear when full and in second when it is empty.

TOP: **The rear of a BMP-1 with all its doors and hatches open. The bulbous rear doors doubled as fuel tanks for the vehicle. The four large hatches are fully open, each hatch acting as an exit for two men. The pistol ports just above the track skirt are in the closed position. On the rear of the door is storage for two metal track chocks.** ABOVE: **The full complement of the vehicle can be clearly seen. On the left is the driver, behind him is the vehicle commander, in the turret is the gunner, and in the rear of the vehicle is the eight-man infantry section.** LEFT: **A close-up of the Sagger AT missile. The loading hatch is just large enough for the missile to be pushed up and on to its launching rail.**

| BMP-1 Infantry Fighting Vehicle |
|---|
| **Country:** USSR |
| **Entered service:** 1966 |
| **Crew:** 3 plus 8 infantry |
| **Weight:** 12,802kg/12.6 tons |
| **Dimensions:** Length – 6.74m/22ft 1in<br>Height – 2.15m/7ft 1in<br>Width – 2.94m/9ft 8in |
| **Armament:** Main – 1 x 2A28 Grom 73mm/<br>2.87in gun, 1 x coaxial 7.62mm/0.3in<br>PKT machine-gun<br>Secondary – Sagger launch rail and small arms |
| **Armour:** Maximum – 33mm/1.3in |
| **Powerplant:** UTD-20 6-cylinder 224kW/300hp<br>diesel engine |
| **Performance:** Speed – Road 80kph/50mph;<br>Water 6–8kph/4–5mph<br>Range – 500km/311 miles |

# BMP-2 Infantry Fighting Vehicle

The BMP-2 was a development of the BMP-1 and was first seen by the NATO allies in the Moscow Parade of 1982. Several steps were taken to improve on the BMP-1. The new vehicle had a larger two-man turret, the infantry section in the rear was reduced from eight to six men and the vehicle commander was moved from behind the driver's position into the turret next to the gunner to give him better all-round vision.

The driver sits in the front on the left with the radio operator behind and the engine pack next to them. The two-man turret has the vehicle commander on the right and the gunner on the left. The main armament is the 30mm/1.18in 2A42 automatic cannon, which has two rates of fire: slow at 200 rounds per minute and fast at 550 rounds per minute. However, the turret can not remove the fumes from the gun when being fired at the faster speed. A Spandrel anti-tank missile system is mounted on the roof. Twenty-two thousand BMP-2 vehicles were produced between 1990 and 1997.

LEFT: **A BMP-2. The turret is fitted with two clusters of three smoke dischargers. On the rear of the vehicle is a snorkel tube in the stored position. The mounting for the Spandrel AT-5 ATGW is situated on the roof of the turret at the rear.**

## BMP-2 Infantry Fighting Vehicle

**Country:** USSR
**Entered service:** 1981
**Crew:** 3 plus 6 infantry
**Weight:** 14,224kg/14 tons
**Dimensions:** Length – 6.74m/22ft 1in
　　　Height – 2.45m/8ft
　　　Width – 3.15m/10ft 4in
**Armament:** Main – 2A42 30mm/1.18in cannon, and coaxial 7.62mm/0.3in machine-gun
　　　Secondary – Spandrel launcher and small arms
**Armour:** Classified
**Powerplant:** UTD-20 6-cylinder 224kW/300hp diesel engine
**Performance:** Speed – Road 65kph/40mph;
　　　Water 7kph/4mph
　　　Range – 600km/373 miles

# BMP-3 Infantry Fighting Vehicle

LEFT: **The rear of the BMP-3. The back of this vehicle has been redesigned and the fuel tanks have been removed from the doors and placed inside the vehicle under the floor of the troop compartment.**

## BMP-3 Infantry Fighting Vehicle

**Country:** USSR
**Entered service:** 1989
**Crew:** 3 plus 7 infantry
**Weight:** 19,304kg/19 tons
**Dimensions:** Length – 7.14m/23ft 5in
　　　Height – 2.3m/7ft 7in
　　　Width – 3.15m/10ft 4in
**Armament:** Main – 1 x 2A70 100mm/3.94in gun, 1 x 2A72 30mm/1.18in cannon, and 1 x 7.62mm/0.3in machine-gun
　　　Secondary – Small arms
**Armour:** Classified
**Powerplant:** UTD-29M 10-cylinder multi-fuel 373kW/500hp engine
**Performance:** Speed – Road 70kph/44mph;
　　　Water 10kph/6mph
　　　Range – 600km/373 miles

The BMP-3 is a radical new design and was first seen in 1990. In 2005, it represented the heaviest armed infantry fighting vehicle then in service but a number of ill-conceived improvements to the BMP concept have resulted in this vehicle having a very poor design. Experience has also shown that the vehicle has low battlefield survivability.

The driver is still seated in the front but is now located in the centre, under the main gun. The turret is fitted with three weapons: a 100mm/3.94in 2A70 gun (a totally new design, not the same as the one fitted to the T-55), a 30mm/1.18in cannon and a 7.62mm/0.3in machine-gun. The BMP-3 has a new engine which is now positioned under the floor in the rear of the vehicle together with some of the fuel cells. It is propelled in the water by two water jets mounted at the rear of the vehicle.

The BMP-3 is in service with seven different countries and by 1997 Russia had 200 BMP-3s on active service. However, the vehicle is not well-liked and this could explain why production has been so slow.

LEFT: **A Bradley at speed. The driver's hatch is in the half-open position to give improved vision. The large engine intake grills can be seen on the glacis plate.** ABOVE: **The boxes on the side of the turret are for the twin TOW AT missile system. The upper part of the track and hull sides have been fitted with appliqué armour. The storage box on the rear of the vehicle is for camouflage netting.**

# Bradley M2 Infantry Fighting Vehicle

In the mid 1960s the American Army required a new infantry vehicle, which they wanted to out-perform the Soviet BMP-1, to replace the M113. Until 1977 no development vehicle had been produced which proved to be adequate and so the projects were dropped. In that year, two new vehicles were developed – the XM2 (Bradley Infantry Fighting Vehicle) and the XM3 (Bradley Cavalry Vehicle). However, in 1978 both of these vehicles were condemned by the General Accounting Office as being too slow, too high, having a very poor engine and insufficient armour. Some of these problems, but not all, were rectified in further development and in 1981 the first production vehicles were handed over to the army.

Initially, the American Army had a requirement for 6,800 Bradley M2s, but this has since been reduced. The hull of the M2 is made of all-welded aluminium armour which is further protected with spaced laminated armour. The driver of the vehicle sits at the front on the left-hand side, with the engine on the right-hand side. The turret is mounted on the top of the vehicle in the middle with the commander on the right and the gunner on the left. The main armament is the 25mm/0.98in M242 chain gun with a coaxial M240 7.62mm/0.3in machine-gun. The gunner can select single shot or two different burst rates and, as it is fully stabilized in all plains, the gun can be laid and fired on the move. Two TOW missiles, with a range of 3,750m/12,300ft, are mounted on the outside of the turret. The Bradley has a swimming ability and this is effected by using a flotation screen that is permanently fitted to the vehicle. The rear of the vehicle holds six infantrymen, each with a firing port to the side or rear of the vehicle. The NBC system is limited to the three-man crew and does not provide protection for the infantry in the rear.

The Bradley is still very heavily criticized by the men who use it in the field, in spite of numerous upgrades since coming into service.

ABOVE: **The driver's hatch is in the fully open position on this vehicle. The large rear ramp is in the down position. The last appliqué armour plate is folded up; this allows access to the tracks without removing the armour.**

## Bradley M2 Infantry Fighting Vehicle

**Country:** USA
**Entered service:** 1981
**Crew:** 3 plus 6 infantry
**Weight:** 22,260 kg/22 tons
**Dimensions:** Length – 6.47m/21ft 3in
 Height – 3m/9ft 10in
 Width – 3.28m/10ft 9in
**Armament:** Main – M242 25mm/0.98in cannon, and coaxial M240 7.62 mm/0.3in machine-gun
 Secondary – Small arms
**Armour:** Classified
**Powerplant:** Cummins VTA-903T turbocharged 8-cylinder 373kW/500hp diesel engine
**Performance:** Speed – Road 61kph/38mph; Water 6.4kph/4mph
 Range – 400km/249 miles

LEFT: **A radiological-chemical reconnaissance BRDM-2 car. The boxes at the rear of the car carry a number of pennants that are used to mark a safe lane through contaminated ground.**

# BRDM-2 Armoured Car

The same team that designed the original BRDM armoured car were used to develop the BRDM-2. The process started in 1962, using their experience and the basic BRDM as a starting point. The new design had to incorporate several improvements such as better road and cross-country performance, full amphibious capability and heavier, turret-mounted armament. The new BRDM-2 entered production in 1963 and was first seen in a public parade in 1966. Production finished in 1989 but it is still in service with the Russian Army and the armed forces of some 55 other countries.

The BRDM-2 is an all-welded steel construction, with the driver and commander sitting side by side in the front of the vehicle. The turret, which is manually operated, is the same as that fitted to the BTR-60PB, BTR-70 and the OT-64 model 2A, and is armed with a 14.55mm/0.57in heavy machine-gun and a coaxial 7.62mm/0.3in machine-gun. The vehicle is equipped with a central tyre pressure system as fitted to all Soviet wheeled vehicles which allows the driver to increase or decrease the tyre pressure depending on the terrain encountered. Between the main wheels are a set of smaller chain-driven belly wheels which drop down when operating on soft ground. The engine is mounted in the rear of the vehicle to help improve the cross-country performance.

There are six variations of the basic vehicle, the most common being the BRDM-2 with Sagger ATGWs, which was first used in combat during the 1973

ABOVE LEFT: **A BRDM-1. The driver and commander sit in the front of this vehicle. The vehicle commander's position has been fitted with a single 12.7mm/0.5in machine-gun. The basic vehicle has a crew of five.**
LEFT: **A BRDM-2 armed with Sagger AT missiles. These missiles are in the raised ready-to-launch position. When not in use, the missiles are retracted into the vehicle.**

Middle East campaigns. In this variant the turret and the hull top are removed and replaced by a six-rail Sagger launcher in which the armoured cover, missile rails, missiles and firing mechanism are all one unit. When travelling the missiles are stored in the body of the vehicle but in action the entire unit is raised into the firing position. Other vehicle variants include a command version, radiological-chemical reconnaissance car, Swatter-B and Spandrel ATGW vehicles and the SA-9 Gaskin AA system.

The BRDM-2 has proved to be a very rugged and reliable design and is expected to be in service for many more years with a number of countries.

## BRDM-2 Armoured Car

**Country:** USSR
**Entered service:** 1964
**Crew:** 4
**Weight:** 7,000kg/6.9 tons
**Dimensions:** Length – 5.75m/18ft 10in
    Height – 2.31m/7ft 7in
    Width – 2.35m/7ft 9in
**Armament:** Main – 14.55mm/0.57in KPVT machine-gun, and coaxial 7.62mm/0.3in PKT machine-gun
    Secondary – Small arms
**Armour:** Maximum – 14mm/0.55in
**Powerplant:** GAZ 41 8-cylinder 105kw/140hp petrol engine
**Performance:** Speed – Road 100kph/62mph;
    Water 10kph/6mph
    Range – 750km/466 miles

# BTR-60 Armoured Personnel Carrier

LEFT: **The first vehicle on the flat car is a BTR-60PU command car. This is a conversion of the basic BTR-60PB. The PU version is fitted with several radios and a 10m/32ft 10in aerial, which on this vehicle is folded down and stored on the top of the vehicle.** BELOW: **Two BTR-60PB vehicles being unloaded from tank landing craft during a Soviet exercise. The vehicle in front has one of the large hatches above the crew compartment open.**

The BTR-60 was developed in the late 1950s to replace the BTR-152. It entered service in 1960 with the Motorized Rifle Divisions and was first seen by the West during the Moscow Parade of November 1961. Each Rifle Division is equipped with 417 of these vehicles although some have since had their BTR-60s replaced by the BMP-1.

The BTR-60P, an open-topped vehicle, was the first model released. This was only in service for a few years and was quickly relegated to a training role. In 1961, the new BTR-60PA entered service. This had a covered armoured roof, but was quickly improved upon when the BTR-60PB entered service in 1965. The 60PB was the same as the PA except that it was fitted with the same turret as the BRDM and mounted a single 14.55mm/0.57in KPV machine-gun. This was the last improvement on the

basic Infantry Carrier, the other versions produced all being command vehicles.

The hull of the BTR-60 is an all-welded steel construction. The driver sits on the left and vehicle commander on the right in the front of the vehicle, while behind them is the one-man turret. Behind the turret area is the infantry accommodation which seats 14 men on bench seats. At the rear of the vehicle is the engine area, which houses the twin engines of the vehicle. The BTR-60 is an 8-wheel drive. The forward four wheels are steerable and each tyre is attached to a central tyre pressure system that is controlled by the driver. The vehicle has a good cross-country ability but debussing under fire is extremely exposed for the infantry, as they have to emerge from hatches in the top of the vehicle or through two small hatches, one on either side.

The BTR-60 was slowly phased out of service to be replaced by the BTR-70 from 1979 onwards. Total production was about 25,000 new vehicles, excluding the upgrades carried out on the early models to bring them up to BTR-60PB standard. These vehicles are still found in service with some countries of the former Soviet bloc.

### BTR-60PB APC

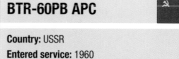

**Country:** USSR
**Entered service:** 1960
**Crew:** 2 plus 14 infantry
**Weight:** 10,300kg/10.1 tons
**Dimensions:** Length – 7.56m/24ft 10in
    Height – 2.31m/7ft 7in
    Width – 2.83m/9ft 3in
**Armament:** Main – 14.55mm/0.57in KPV
    machine-gun
    Secondary – Small arms
**Armour:** Maximum – 9mm/0.354in
**Powerplant:** 2 x GAZ 49B 6-cylinder 67kW/90hp
    petrol engines
**Performance:** Speed – Road 80kph/50mph;
    Water 10kph/6.2mph
    Range – 500km/311 miles

RIGHT: **The driver's and vehicle commander's front hatches are open. The hatch halfway down the vehicle can be used as an exit point. The trim vane is in the stowed position under the nose of the vehicle.**

# BTR-70 Armoured Personnel Carrier

LEFT: **A column of BTR-70 APC vehicles out on exercise. The four large rubber wheels can clearly been seen on these vehicles. All the wheels are connected to a central tyre pressure system operated by the driver.** BELOW: **Between the second and third wheels is a small hatch which troops can use to exit the vehicle, but only when stopped. The pistol ports in the side of the crew compartment can also be seen.**

While the BMP was the most revolutionary armoured vehicle developed by the Soviet Union, the BTR-70 was the least radical as it was a straight evolution of the BTR-60. Development started in 1971 with production commencing in 1972. It entered service in 1976, but was not seen until 1980 when it was spotted in the November Moscow Parade. The delays in production were a result of a catastrophic fire at the engine factory.

The hull of the vehicle is longer than the BTR-60 while the front and rear were widened to give the wheels better protection. The hull was an all-welded steel construction, with the driver and commander in the front and behind them two infantrymen who could use the forward-facing pistol ports to cover the front of the vehicle and debussing infantry. Behind them was the turret area which was the same as that fitted to the BTR-60 and was operated by one infantryman. There were plans to fit the BMP turret to the vehicle but this proved to be too expensive and would have required a major redesign.

Behind the turret are two bench seats for six infantry who sit in two rows of three facing outwards so they could use the pistol ports in the side of the vehicle. Behind the infantry area is the engine compartment.

The BTR-70 retained the twin-engine layout of the BTR-60 except that one engine powered the first and third wheels while the other powered the second and fourth wheels, so that if the vehicle lost an engine at least it could limp off the battlefield unlike the BTR-60 which would go round in circles. Between the second and third wheels on each side is a small crew hatch for the infantry to debus, but the vehicle has to stop for

this to happen otherwise the soldiers would be crushed by the wheels.

During the fighting in Afghanistan the BTR-70 showed that it was very vulnerable to attack from the side by heavy machine-guns and rocket launchers such as the RPG7. A number of field modifications were carried out to increase the armour and extra weapons were fitted such as the AGS-17 grenade launcher.

## BTR-70 APC

**Country:** USSR
**Entered service:** 1976
**Crew:** 2 plus 9 infantry
**Weight:** 11,481kg/11.3 tons
**Dimensions:** Length – 7.54m/24ft 9in
  Height – 2.23m/7ft 4in
  Width – 2.8m/9ft 2in
**Armament:** Main – 14.55mm/0.57in KPVT
  machine-gun, and coaxial 7.62mm/0.3in
  PKT machine-gun
  Secondary – Small arms
**Armour:** Maximum – 10mm/0.394in
**Powerplant:** 2 x ZMZ-4905 6-cylinder
  172kW/230hp petrol engines
**Performance:** Speed – 80kph/50mph
  Range – 600km/370 miles

ABOVE: **The boat shape of the hull shows up well on this vehicle. One of the two large exhausts can be seen at the rear of the vehicle.**

LEFT: **The turret of this BTR-80 has a bank of six smoke dischargers fitted to the rear. Just in the picture is the hydro water-jet hatch which propels this type of vehicle in the water. The height of the rear of the vehicle has been raised.** ABOVE: **The new side door can be seen on this BTR-80. This allowed the crew to leave the vehicle while still on the move as they can jump clear of the wheels.**

# BTR-80 Armoured Personnel Carrier

The BTR-70 did not cure all the deficiencies of the BTR-60, which had become evident during the fighting in Afghanistan. It simply displayed the shortcomings of the reliance on the conservative development of armoured vehicles. The replacement for the BTR-70, initially called the GAZ 5903, started development in 1982. It passed its trials and was renamed the BTR-80, with production starting in 1984.

The three main differences to the BTR-70 were the engine, the crew exit doors and the turret. The twin-engine configuration was dropped in favour of a single large diesel engine, which simplified the automotive train and made maintenance easier. Clam-shell doors were fitted to the sides of the vehicle

instead of small hatches. When the doors are opened, the bottom one forms a step which drops down between the second and third road-wheels. The BTR-80 does not have to halt to allow the infantry to debus: the clam-shell doors are opened and the men leap off the step one at a time hoping to miss the wheels. It is consequently known as the "death step". The last major change was the turret. The gun was designed to allow elevation to 60 degrees, as it had been found in Afghanistan that the gun could not be elevated high enough to sweep the hills. This also gives the vehicle some anti-aircraft ability to deal with helicopters. The BTR-80 has two firing ports in the front and three down each side for the infantry to use, and is fully

amphibious with a single water jet mounted in the rear. The steering is applied to the front four wheels and the vehicle is fitted with a full NBC system and night-vision equipment. It is in service with some 20 countries.

One version of the BTR-80 is the BREM-80 (*Bronirovannaya Remontno-Evakuatsionnaya Mashina*) Armoured Recovery Vehicle, which was developed to recover damaged wheeled vehicles from the battlefield. There is a nose-mounted spade to secure the vehicle during winching operations, a small jib crane on the roof and a large "A" frame that can be fitted to the front of the BREM for engine changes.

RIGHT: **The trim vane is in its new stored position lying flat on the glacis plate. The vehicle commander is standing in his position with his hatch opening to the front of the vehicle. The exhaust system on the BTR-80 now runs almost horizontal along the rear of the raised engine compartment.**

## BTR-80 APC

**Country:** USSR
**Entered service:** 1984
**Crew:** 3 plus 7 infantry
**Weight:** 13,614kg/13.4 tons
**Dimensions:** Length – 7.5m/24ft 7in
  Height – 2.45m/8ft
  Width – 2.9m/9ft 6in
**Armament:** Main – 14.55mm/0.57in KPVT machine-gun, and coaxial 7.62mm/0.3in PKT machine-gun
  Secondary – Small arms
**Armour:** Maximum – 10mm/0.394in
**Powerplant:** KAMAZ 7403 8-cylinder 194kW/260hp diesel engine
**Performance:** Speed – 80kph/50mph
  Range – 600km/370 miles

# BTR-152V1 Armoured Personnel Carrier

The BTR-152 was the first Soviet APC to be developed after World War II. The process started at the end of World War II and the vehicle entered service in 1950, but was first seen by the West during the Moscow Parade of 1951. Initially the BTR-152 was developed using the ZIL-151 2.5-ton truck but this was later changed to the ZIL-157 truck.

The BTR-152 has the engine located at the front of the vehicle and behind this is an open-topped compartment with accommodation for two crew and 17 infantry. The infantry in the rear of the vehicle sit on bench seats behind the crew compartment, while the driver and commander sit in the front with the driver on the left. There are eight firing ports, three down each side and one in each of the rear doors. The early vehicles had no NBC equipment, night-driving equipment or amphibious capability but some of the later variants such as the BTR-152V3

were fitted with a central tyre pressure system, and a night-driving infrared driving light.

The BTR-152K came into service from 1961. This has a full armoured roof with two large hatches, one in the front and one in the rear, each with a machine-gun mount. All the other improvements from the early versions were fitted to this mark, but still no NBC system. There were three machine-gun mounts in total, one over the driver and commander's position which would take a heavy 12.7mm/0.5in machine-gun and one 7.62mm/0.3in SGMB machine-gun mounted on each side of the vehicle. In addition to being used as an infantry carrier, the BTR-152 was also used as an artillery tractor, mortar carrier and a basic load carrier. One command vehicle version of the BTR-152 was produced as well as three anti-aircraft versions. The first of these mounted a

ABOVE: **The truck origins of the vehicle chassis can be clearly seen. The driver is entering his position in the vehicle. The pistol ports in the side of the crew compartment are visible. The main 12.7mm/0.5in heavy machine-gun mount is sited above the driver's position.**

twin 14.55mm/0.57in machine-gun turret, the second had a quadruple 12.7mm/0.5in machine-gun turret and the last version had twin 23mm/0.91in cannon. The Egyptians have fitted the Czechoslovak M53 turret to some of their BTR-152s.

The BTR-152 has been replaced in the Soviet Army but still remains in service with many countries.

## BTR-152V1 APC

**Country:** USSR
**Entered service:** 1950
**Crew:** 2 plus 17 infantry
**Weight:** 8,738kg/8.6 tons
**Dimensions:** Length – 6.55m/21ft 6in
Height – 2.36m/7ft 9in
Width – 2.32m/7ft 7in
**Armament:** Main – 12.7mm/0.5in DShKM machine-gun, and 2 x 7.62mm/0.3in SGMB machine-guns
Secondary – Small arms
**Armour:** Maximum – 14mm/0.55in
**Powerplant:** ZIL-123 6-cylinder 82kW/110hp petrol engine
**Performance:** Speed – 75kph/47mph
Range – 600km/373 miles

LEFT: **A BTR-40 APC. This was the second vehicle type to be built by the Soviet Union after World War II. It had a crew of two and could carry eight men in the back. There is a 12.7mm/0.5in machine-gun mount above the driver's cab.**

# Cascavel EE-9 Mk IV Armoured Car

The Cascavel was designed by ENGESA to meet the requirements of the Brazilian Army, with design work starting in July 1970. The first prototype was completed in 1970 and a pre-production order for ten vehicles was placed and delivered between 1972 and 1973. Production began in 1974 with the vehicle entering Brazilian Army service in the same year. These early vehicles (Mk I) were fitted with M3 37mm/1.46in turrets taken from the now-redundant American light tanks used by the Brazilian Army. The second version (Mk II) of the vehicle was fitted with the Hispano-Suiza H90 turret. The EE-9 and the EE-11 APC have many parts in common and a lot of these are standard commercial parts.

The hull of the vehicle is made from spaced armour with the outer layer having dual hardness. This outer layer is constructed of a hardened steel sheet

and a softer steel rolled together to form one single dual-hardened steel sheet. The driver sits in the front on the left-hand side with the two-man turret behind him and the engine in the rear. The rear wheels are mounted on an ENGESA Boomerang walking beam suspension arm that allows the vehicle to have all four wheels in contact with the ground at all times. The vehicle is a 6x6 and is fitted with run-flat tyres. Even after being fully deflated, the EE-9 can travel on them for 100km/62 miles before they have to be replaced.

Anticipating the finite supply of M3 turrets, ENGESA started to manufacture their own turrets and guns. These ENGESA ET-90 turrets and EC-90 guns were fitted to the EE-9 once the M3 turrets had run out, creating the Mk III. The Mk IV was the next version to enter production in 1979. This saw significant improvements over previous versions

ABOVE LEFT: **This is a Cascavel on parade in Venezuela. Both the vehicle commander and the turret gunner are standing in the top of their turret position. The commander's cupola is fitted with a machine-gun.**
ABOVE: **The Cascavel climbing a steep slope. The very flat rear of the vehicle and turret sides can be clearly seen. The rear of the turret on this Brazilian vehicle has been fitted with a storage basket.**

with the installation of a new engine and the fitting of a central tyre pressure system controlling all wheels similar to that on Soviet vehicles. The Mk V is the last variation and this is powered by a German Mercedes-Benz diesel rather than the American engine of the Mk IV.

## Cascavel EE-9 Mk IV Armoured Car

**Country:** Brazil
**Entered service:** 1979
**Crew:** 3
**Weight:** 13,411kg/13.2 tons
**Dimensions:** Length – 6.2m/20ft 4in
  Height – 2.68m/9ft 9in
  Width – 2.64m/8ft 8in
**Armament:** Main – EC-90 90mm/3.54in gun, and coaxial 7.62mm/0.3in machine-gun
  Secondary – 12.7mm/0.5in anti-aircraft machine-gun
**Armour:** Maximum – 16mm/0.63in
**Powerplant:** Detroit Diesel model 6V-53N 6-cylinder 158kW/212hp diesel engine
**Performance:** Speed – 100kph/62mph
  Range – 880km/547 miles

LEFT: **The vehicle commander's position has been fitted with a 7.62mm/0.3in machine-gun and the vehicle is fitted with two whip aerials. At the rear of the turret on each side is a cluster of smoke dischargers, one set of which is visible here.**

# Commando V-150 Armoured Personnel Carrier

ABOVE: **This is one of the prototype development vehicles, and is fitted with a fixed turret. The large side door is in the open position with the top of the door folded back against the hull and the bottom of the door acting as a step.**

The Cadillac Gage Company started development of the Commando in 1962 as a private venture, with the first prototype being finished in March 1963. The first production vehicles entered service in 1964. The Commando saw extensive service with the American Army and with the American Air Force during the Vietnam War. It was deployed as a convoy escort for both services and also as an airfield defence vehicle.

The Commando is very much a mix-and-match vehicle: the customer can chose one of several bodies and one of about 14 different turrets. Its American designation is the M706. The first

type of vehicle was the V-100, which was followed very shortly by the V-200 and finally the V-150 which came into service in 1971 and replaced both the V-100 and V-200. The V-150S entered production in 1985. The V-100 is very similar to the V-150 except that the V-100 has a petrol engine while the V-150's engine is a diesel. The V-200 was a beefed-up version, much larger than ether of the other two vehicles.

The V-150 is an all-welded steel construction and provides the crew with protection from up to 7.62mm/0.3in bullets and shrapnel. The driver sits at the front on the left-hand side and, depending on the version, the vehicle commander's seat is next to the driver. Behind them is the main crew compartment that can be fitted with a variety of turrets and can even have an open top. The one-man turrets have a single hatch in the top and are armed with a variety of machine-guns up to 20mm/0.79in, either mounted in pairs or singly. The two-man turret has two hatches and the armament ranges from 20mm/0.79in up to 90mm/3.54in guns. There are three doors in the main hull, one on each side and one in the rear. The top half of the door folds back flush with the vehicle while the bottom folds down and forms a step for the infantry to clear the vehicle and its wheels. There are eight pistol ports fitted to the vehicle, two in the front and three down each side. The maximum number of infantry that can be carried in the vehicle is 12 but

LEFT: **The rear of the Commando prototype vehicle showing the large rear exit door. The top of the door flips up and the bottom drops down to form a step.**

LEFT: **The good ground clearance can be clearly seen. This turret can be fitted with either a single or twin 7.62mm/0.3in machine-gun.** ABOVE: **This Commando is being used as a reconnaissance vehicle. It is armed with a single machine-gun. One of the men is operating from inside the vehicle but to have a better vision has opened the top half of the hull door.** BELOW: **A number of Commando vehicles have been sold to police forces around the world. They act as internal security or riot control vehicles.**

this does vary depending on the version. The engine is mounted in the rear of the V-150 on the left-hand side with a corridor on the right leading to the rear door. In this corridor are two seating positions while above the corridor is a small circular hatch that opens towards the front of the vehicle and has a pintle mount for a 7.62mm/0.3in machine-gun to cover the rear of the vehicle.

The mortar vehicle and the TOW missile vehicle have a raised section added to the roof in place of the turret. This is fitted with two folding hatches that run the length of the raised area and fold to the sides of the vehicle. The 81mm/3.19in mortar is mounted in the middle of the crew compartment on a turntable and can be traversed through 360 degrees. Its minimum range is 150m/492ft with a maximum range of 4,400m/14,435ft. There are also four pintle mounts for 7.62mm/0.3in machine-guns. The vehicle has a crew of five and also carries 62 mortar bombs. The hatches for the TOW vehicle open front and back; it can carry seven missiles and

has a crew of four. There is also a command version built using this basic type of hull and a police riot vehicle has also been developed for several American police departments. An armoured recovery version of the V-150 has also been developed and it is designed for the recovery of broken down or damaged light armoured vehicles. This is fitted with a heavy duty winch and "A" frame that is attached to the front of the vehicle and folds back across the top of the crew compartment when not required. A large number of these vehicles are still in service.

Some 4,000 of the V-150s have been built and are in service with 21 countries. The only country to purchase the V-200 was Singapore and the V-100 was only purchased by the USA.

RIGHT: **The driver's and vehicle commander's vision ports are protected by armoured covers. The vehicle also has a number of vision ports in the side of the vehicle. The open fixed turret of this vehicle has been improved and turned into a command turret.**

## Commando V-150 APC

**Country:** USA
**Entered service:** 1971
**Crew:** 2 crew plus 10 infantry
**Weight:** 9,550kg/9.4 tons
**Dimensions:** Length – 5.68m/19ft 8in
    Height – 2.43m/8ft
    Width – 2.26m/7ft 5in
**Armament:** Main – Various
    Secondary – Small arms
**Armour:** Classified
**Powerplant:** Chrysler V-504 8-cylinder
    151kW/202hp diesel engine
**Performance:** Speed – 88kph/55mph
    Range – 950km/600 miles

LEFT: **The hatches over the troop compartment have been folded back against the hull of the vehicle, with the men sitting in the raised position. The vehicle commander is operating the machine-gun over his position.**

# DAF YP-408 Armoured Personnel Carrier

DAF (*Van Doorne's Automobielfabrieken*) started development of the YP-408 carrier in 1956 to meet a Dutch Army requirement. The first prototypes were finished in 1958 and were powered by an American Hercules JXLD petrol engine, but this was changed in the production model. The vehicle went through a number of modifications and finally an order was placed for 750 vehicles with the first carriers being delivered to the

Dutch Army in 1964. By 1988, the YP-408 had been phased out of service with the Dutch being replaced by the YPR-765.

The hull is an all-welded construction with the engine, transmission and radiator in the front. The driver and the commander/gunner are placed side by side behind the engine with the driver on the left. The gunner's hatch cover is in two parts that only open to the vertical position and so provide some protection

when manning the machine-gun. The troop compartment is in the rear of the vehicle and holds ten men, who sit down the sides of the vehicle facing each other with their legs interlocking. Entry and exit from the crew compartment is by twin doors in the rear, each door having a single firing port in it.

The YP-408 uses many of the same components as the YP-328 (6x6) truck, but this vehicle is an 8x6 layout. It has power steering and steers using the front two axles, the second axle being unpowered. The YP-408 is fitted with dual air and hydraulic brakes, and the tyres can be driven on for 50km/31 miles when punctured. The vehicle is not fitted with an NBC system and is not amphibious, but it can be fitted with infrared night-driving equipment.

There were several variations on the basic vehicle. The two command versions had one row of seats removed and a map table in their place. Other variants include: an ambulance; an armoured supply carrier; a mortar tractor which had a total crew of seven, towed the 120mm/4.72in mortar and carried 50 mortar bombs; an anti-tank vehicle armed with TOW missiles; and a ground radar vehicle.

MIDDLE LEFT: **The gunner's hatch covers are fully open as they only open to this vertical position. The top of the troop compartment has six large hatches recessed into it.** LEFT: **The second axle from the front can be raised and locked into position clear of the ground. This is so the wheels can be used as spares for the other wheel positions.**

## DAF YP-408 APC

**Country:** Netherlands
**Entered service:** 1964
**Crew:** 2 plus 10 infantry
**Weight:** 11,989kg/11.8 tons
**Dimensions:** Length – 6.2m/20ft 4in
    Height – 1.55m/5ft 11in
    Width – 2.4m/7ft 9in
**Armament:** Main – 12.7mm/0.5in heavy
    machine-gun
    Secondary – Small arms
**Armour:** Maximum – 15mm/0.59in
**Powerplant:** DAF Model DS-575 6-cylinder
    123kW/165hp diesel engine
**Performance:** Speed – 80kph/50mph
    Range – 500km/310 miles

LEFT: **The left rear of the turret houses the hydraulic motor for the elevation and traversing of the turret. This vehicle has been sheeted up as it is not operational.** ABOVE: **The armoured cab of the DANA houses the driver and vehicle commander. Their armoured hatches are in the open position. All the wheels are connected to a central tyre pressure system operated by the driver. The gun layer sits behind the large hatch on the left of the turret.**

# DANA 152mm Self-Propelled Howitzer

The DANA 152mm/5.98in SPG was first seen in 1980 but development had been taking place during the 1970s, using an extensively modified Tatra 815 (8x8) chassis. A wheeled chassis was selected rather the normal tracked chassis as maintenance is easier and the vehicle is significantly cheaper to produce. Czechoslovakia also has a very good road network making the cross-country capability less important. However, the DANA has a more than adequate cross-country ability for medium-range artillery support for infantry and armour. By 1994, 750 DANA vehicles had been built, and it has been sold to Poland, Russia and Libya, besides being supplied to the

Czechoslovak and, after the break-up of Czechoslovakia, Slovak armies.

The engine on the original Tatra 815 is in the front but on the DANA it was moved to the rear of the vehicle. The lightly armoured cab is protected by armour just 7.62mm/0.3in thick, making it only bullet and light shell-splinter proof. It is situated very low down on the chassis at the front of the vehicle. The driver and one other crew member sit side by side in the cab along with the main radio. The driver and co-driver have large individual toughened glass windscreens that are protected in action by large steel shutters that fold down and cover them. The turret has a crew of three including the vehicle commander

together with a gunner and loader. It is divided into two parts; the left-hand side contains all the optics and fire control systems with the ammunition handler on the right-hand side. Access to the turret is via two doors, one on each side, and it can traverse through 225 degrees to each side being restricted due to internal cables. The turret holds 60 rounds of ammunition and the gun has a fully automatic loading system.

A new version of the DANA called the Zuzanna has been developed, which has been fitted with a NATO-standard calibre 155mm/6.1in gun. The Slovak Army have 16 of these new vehicles in service at present and are due to take delivery of further units each year until 2010.

LEFT: **The gun barrel on this vehicle is at maximum elevation. Between the second and third axle is a stabilizer on each side of the vehicle with a third one at the rear of the vehicle. Five countries operate the DANA, four of which are at present upgrading to the ZUZANA.**

## DANA 152mm SPG

**Country:** Czechoslovakia
**Entered service:** 1980
**Crew:** 5
**Weight:** 29,261kg/28.8 tons
**Dimensions:** Length – 11.15m/36ft 7in
  Height – 2.85m/9ft 4in
  Width – 3m/9ft 10in
**Armament:** Main – 152mm/5.98in howitzer
  Secondary – 12.7mm/0.5in DshKM machine-gun
**Armour:** Maximum – 12.7mm/0.5in
**Powerplant:** Tatra 2-939-34 12-cylinder
  257kW/345hp diesel engine
**Performance:** Speed – 80kph/50mph
  Range – 700km/435 miles

LEFT: **This is a prototype vehicle of the Urutu. The hull sides of the car are vertical until halfway up the vehicle from which point they slope slightly inwards. There is a large single door in the rear.**

# ENGESA EE-11 Urutu Armoured Personnel Carrier

The EE-11 was designed and developed by ENGESA in January 1970 and the first prototype was delivered in July 1970. Once the vehicle had passed its trials, an order was placed in 1974 by the Brazilian Army for the Brazilian Marines.

The EE-11 shares many of the automotive components of the EE-9 armoured car which was developed at the same time. The hull of the vehicle is made from spaced armour with the outer layer having a dual hardness. The outer layer is made up of a hardened steel sheet and a softer steel rolled together to form one single dual-hardened steel sheet. The driver sits in the front on the left-hand side with the engine on the right. The air inlet louvers are on the top of the vehicle next to the driver, with the exhaust on the right-hand side. This amphibious vehicle has been upgraded seven times and each improvement has been to the engine. From the Mk VI onwards, the propellers that propel the EE-11 in the water have been removed as the wheels of the vehicle work well enough in the water to move it forward. There is also a trim vane, hydraulically operated by the driver, fitted to the glacis plate.

The vehicle can be fitted with a range of turrets, but the basic Urutu has a pintle mount for either a 7.62mm/0.3in or a 12.7mm/0.5in machine-gun, and five firing ports down each side and one in the rear door. When fitted with any turret from the ET-20 up to the ET-90, the number of firing ports each side of the vehicle is reduced to two with one in the rear door. The crew compartment is behind the gun position and in the basic form carries 12 men although when larger turrets are mounted only four men can be carried. The men sit down the sides of the vehicle with five men on each side and a two-man bench across the top of the troop area behind the turret area. The rear door can be operated by the driver from his position, to make pick-up quicker and safer for the infantry. The two side doors are used for debussing or loading in a peaceful area.

LEFT: **The exhaust system is fitted to the right-hand side of the vehicle above the side door. The trim vane is folded back against the glacis plate, and the headlights are recessed into the hull front. There are several pistol ports down the side of the vehicle. The travel in the suspension system can be clearly seen.**

## EE-11 Urutu APC Mk VII

**Country:** Brazil
**Entered service:** 1974
**Crew:** 1 plus 12 infantry
**Weight:** 14,000kg/13.8 tons
**Dimensions:** Length – 6.1m/20ft
    Height – 2.9m/9ft 6in
    Width – 2.69m/8ft 10in
**Armament:** Main – 12.7mm/0.5in machine-gun
    Secondary – Small arms
**Armour:** Classified
**Powerplant:** Detroit Diesel 6V-53T 6-cylinder 194kW/260hp diesel engine
**Performance:** Speed – Road 105kph/65mph;
    Water 8kph/5mph
    Range – 850km/528 miles

LEFT: **This Ferret Mk 1 has a large storage basket fitted to the rear hull above the engine. Behind the storage bin between the wheels is an escape hatch. When opened, the hatch and storage bin drop away from the vehicle.** ABOVE: **The driver's position in this Ferret armoured car. The dashboard is split into two with the steering wheel in the middle. The handbrake is just in front of the driver's seat. The driver has one large vision block above the steering wheel with smaller ones to the side.**

# Ferret Mk 1 Scout Car

In 1947, the British Army issued a requirement for a replacement for the Daimler Dingo scout car. Daimler consequently started development of the Mk 1 Ferret Scout Car in 1948 with the first prototype being produced in December 1949. The first production Mk 1 Ferrets were delivered in October 1952 and the type would remain in production for 20 years, the final Ferret being produced in 1971. Total production was 4,409 vehicles of which 1,200 were Mk 1s. The Ferret proved to be extremely popular with the men using it and could be found in almost every British Army unit, even units that were not issued with

them. It would remain in service with the British Army until 1994.

The Mk 1 Ferret is a monocoque design made from 30 separate flat plates and is an all-welded construction. The driver is seated in the front with the crew compartment in the middle and the engine in the rear. The crew compartment is open-topped but can be covered by a canvas tilt. The vehicle is a 4x4 layout with steering on the front axle which is not power-assisted. A spare wheel is carried on the left side of the vehicle with storage boxes on the right. The Daimler pre-selective gearbox has five forward and five reverse gears. The Ferret Mk 1

does not carry night-driving infrared lights or NBC system. It can be fitted with deep wading gear but this was a later development that appeared on the Mk 1/3.

The Ferret Mk 1 went through some modifications, the first being in 1959 when the Mk 1/1 came into service. This had increased armour protection, and the open top was covered by a fixed turret, which had a split hatch that folded towards the rear of the vehicle. The Mk 1/3 deep wading gear attaches over the top of the opening or turret area and is a canvas screen that can be raised like an inflated bellows, allowing the vehicle to be submerged (including the driver) with the commander standing in the top of the turret giving directions.

LEFT: **The last combat service for the Ferret was the Gulf War of 1991. This Mk 1 has had a fixed turret placed on the top of the crew area. On each side of the front of the vehicle is a cluster of three smoke dischargers. The storage basket on the rear of the vehicle has been raised.**

## Ferret Mk 1 Scout Car

**Country:** UK
**Entered service:** 1952
**Crew:** 2–3
**Weight:** 4,369kg/4.3 tons
**Dimensions:** Length – 3.84m/12ft 9in
    Height – 1.45m/4ft 9in
    Width – 1.9m/6ft 3in
**Armament:** Main – 7.62mm/0.3in light
    machine-gun
    Secondary – Small arms
**Armour:** Maximum – 16mm/0.63in
**Powerplant:** Rolls-Royce B60 6-cylinder
    87kW/116hp petrol engine
**Performance:** Speed – 93kph/58mph
    Range – 300km/185 miles

LEFT: **The Ferret Mk 2 is fitted with a fully rotating turret armed with a single machine-gun as standard. The exhaust system is fitted on the rear mudguard.**
BELOW: **This Ferret Mk 2/6 has been fitted with the Vigilante AT missile system. This type of vehicle entered service in 1963. The missile boxes increase the overall width of the car. An additional storage box has also been fitted to the side of the vehicle.**

# Ferret Mk 2 Scout Car

The AFV offers an incredible variety of possibilities to the military. It is therefore not surprising that when the British Army issued a requirement for a replacement for the Daimler Dingo in 1947, Daimler developed two variants of the same basic type and both were adopted. Development of the Mk 2 Ferret Scout Car was started in 1948, the first prototype being produced in December 1949. The first production Mk 2 Ferrets were delivered in July 1952, entering service before the Mk 1 Ferrets. It remained in production for 20 years, the final Ferret being produced in 1971. Of the total production of 4,409 vehicles, 1,850 were Mk 2s.

The Mk 2 Ferret is a monocoque design made from 30 separate flat plates and is an all-welded construction. The driver is seated in the front with the turret in the middle and the engine in the rear. The driver has three hatches. The one to the front can be folded down so it lies on the glacis plate and can

then be replaced by a splinter-proof windscreen. There are also hatches on each side of his position, each fitted with a periscope. The turret is very small and cramped and was heavily modified during the trials as it was found that the gunner could accidentally catch his clothing in the trigger and fire the machine-gun. The turret is manually operated as it is small and light and so does not require power. It has two hatches; one in the top that opens forward and gives the gunner some protection as it does not fold flat, and one at the rear of the turret which also folds down to form a seat that the gunner can use. A sighting periscope is fitted in the top of the turret for the gunner to use when in the closed-down position. There are two escape hatches in the Ferret; one behind the spare wheel and the other behind the storage bin on the right-hand side of the vehicle.

LEFT: **The rear vision visors are all open to give the driver a better rear view from the vehicle. Beside the jerry-can on the rear of the car is a fire extinguisher. The small compact size of the vehicle can be clearly seen.**

LEFT: **This Ferret Mk 2/3 has two unditching channels fitted to the front of the car. The aerial on this car is mounted behind one of the clusters of smoke dischargers fitted to the vehicle. A large single searchlight has also been fitted to the side of the turret.** ABOVE: **The driver's and vehicle commander's positions inside the car. The steering wheel is set in a reversed–raked position. The gear selector box is under the steering wheel.**

The engine is fully waterproofed and drive is transmitted to all four wheels by a fluid coupling, five speed pre-selecting epicyclic gearbox and a transfer box, incorporating a forward and reverse mechanism, thus giving the vehicle five forward and five reverse gears and so allowing the vehicle to travel at the same speed in each direction. The Ferret is fully air-transportable and can be delivered by parachute cluster. As a result of this, a lightweight recovery vehicle had to be developed and a number of Ferrets were converted to the role. The Armoured Recovery Vehicle (ARV) conversion came as a kit and could be quickly fitted to a vehicle in the field. This was not an official conversion and remained classified as a local workshop conversion. Another modification that started off as a field modification was the introduction of a storage basket, which was mounted above the engine and was hinged so it could be tilted out of the way to give access to the engine. The basket was fitted to improve the storage of personal equipment which was always a problem.

The Ferret Mk 2 was produced in six different versions. The Mk 2/2 was a local conversion carried out on vehicles in the Far East and consisted of an extension collar fitted between the hull and the turret. The Mk 2/3 was an uparmoured version of the basic Mk 2 and was converted to carry the 7.62mm/0.3in GPMG (General Purpose Machine-Gun). The Mk 2/4 was an uparmoured version of the Mk 2/3 and was fitted with a new fire-fighting system in the crew compartment. The Mk 2/5 was the basic Mk 2 brought up to Mk 2/4 standard. The Ferret Mk 2/6 was fitted with two Vigilante anti-tank missiles, one on each side of the turret, with two spare missiles being carried instead of the spare wheel. The missiles were fired from inside the turret by the vehicle commander.

The Ferret proved to be extremely popular with the men using it and could be found in almost every British Army unit, including units that were not officially issued with them. It would remain in service with the British Army until 1994, some 20 years after it was supposed to retire.

LEFT: **The extra-large storage bin on the side of the vehicle carried two spare missiles. The vehicle commander guides the missiles from this position by a combined sight. The wire guidance box is situated on the top of the turret. Reloading of the missile launchers could be undertaken in less than five minutes.**

## Ferret Mk 2 Scout Car

**Country:** UK
**Entered service:** 1952
**Crew:** 2
**Weight:** 4,369kg/4.3 tons
**Dimensions:** Length – 3.84m/12ft 9in
 Height – 1.88m/6ft 2in
 Width – 1.9m/6ft 3in
**Armament:** Main – 7.62mm/0.3in machine-gun
 Secondary – Small arms
**Armour:** Maximum – 16mm/0.63in
**Powerplant:** Rolls-Royce B60 6-cylinder
 87kW/116hp petrol engine
**Performance:** Speed – 93kph/58mph
 Range – 300km/185 miles

LEFT: **This is the Ferret Mk 5 armed with two Swingfire AT missiles. Spare missiles are carried in storage bins fitted to the vehicle's sides under the turret. The missile boxes are in the maximum elevation firing position.** ABOVE: **This prototype Ferret Mk 4 has the flotation screen fixed in a box structure around the edge of the vehicle. The new water-tight glass-fibre storage box can be seen clearly.**

# Ferret Mk 4 Big Wheeled Scout Car

In 1963 work began on improving the Ferret's automotive and amphibious capabilities, and on providing better storage facilities for the crew's personal equipment. The first six prototypes were converted from Mk 1 vehicles; the basic hull was unchanged but larger tyres were fitted and a flotation screen was carried around the top of the hull. The Mk 4 entered service with the British Army in 1967. None of these vehicles were brand new but were converted Mk 2/3 cars. The last of these conversions were carried out in 1976.

The Mk 4 Ferret is a monocoque design made from 30 separate flat plates and is an all-welded construction. The driver is seated in the front with the turret in the middle and the engine in the rear. The driver's hatch is in the front of the vehicle and can be folded down so it lies on the glacis plate and can then be replaced by a splinter-proof windscreen. During development the larger wheels caused a number of problems with the steering due to the increased weight of the vehicle as the steering was not power-assisted. This would remain a problem with this mark of Ferret. Other improvements on the Mk 4 were enlarged disc brakes and improved suspension. The vehicle was also extended by 38cm/15in to incorporate the flotation screen.

The Mk 5 was a development of the Mk 4, the main difference being the design of the turret. The Mk 5 was to have been built in large numbers but in fact only 50 of these vehicles were made. The new turret had a very flat design and carried four BAC Swingfire anti-tank missiles, two on each side of the centreline. The maximum range of the Swingfire was 4,000m/13,123ft and the missiles were wire-guided and controlled from inside the vehicle by the gunner using a combined sight and controller. Two spare missiles were carried on the vehicle. The turret was made from aluminium armour and could be traversed through 360 degrees but it was not power operated. A 7.62mm/0.3in machine-gun was mounted in the front of it for close protection.

LEFT: **The basic Mk 2/3 was used to produce the Mk 4. The 2/3 was fitted with new brakes, suspension and wheels which gave it a wider track. To make the Mk 5, the suspension changes were made to the 2/6 and a new turret was fitted.**

## Ferret Mk 4 Scout Car

**Country:** UK
**Entered service:** 1967
**Crew:** 2
**Weight:** 5,400kg/5.3 tons
**Dimensions:** Length – 4.1m/13ft 5in
　　Height – 2.34m/7ft 8in
　　Width – 2.13m/7ft
**Armament:** Main – 7.62mm/0.3in light
　　machine-gun
　　Secondary – Small arms
**Armour:** Maximum – 16mm/0.63in
**Powerplant:** Rolls-Royce B60 6-cylinder
　　87kW/116hp petrol engine
**Performance:** Speed – 80kph/50mph
　　Range – 300km/185 miles

# Fox Light Armoured Car

LEFT: **The exhaust is mounted on the rear of the vehicle. There are two side hatches, one on each side of the vehicle below the large two-man turret. These vehicles had a high centre of gravity.**

BELOW: **When the flotation screen is raised, the driver has no vision from his position and so relies on the vehicle commander giving him directions. Transparent screens were fitted to the flotation screen on later models.**

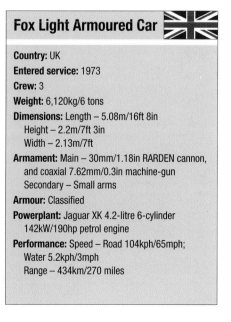

In the 1960s the Fighting Vehicles Research and Development Establishment (FVRDE) developed two vehicles; one was the Combat Vehicle Reconnaissance (Tracked) (CVR(T)) Scorpion and the other the CVR (Wheeled) Fox. Both used the same Jaguar engine. Development started in 1965 and a development contract for 15 prototypes was given to Daimler in 1966. The first vehicle was finished in November 1967 and the last in 1969. Production began in 1972 and the first vehicles entered service in 1973, but this was not to be a replacement for the Ferret. This was the projected role of the Vixen, which was cancelled in 1974.

The Fox was a further development of the late-production Ferret scout car. The

vehicle has an all-welded aluminium hull and turret which gives the crew protection against light and heavy machine-guns and shell splinters. The driver sits in the front of the vehicle with his hatch opening to the right, while the two-man turret is positioned in the middle of the vehicle and is fitted with a 30mm/1.18in RARDEN cannon and a coaxial 7.62mm/0.3in machine-gun. The 4.2-litre Jaguar XK engine is positioned in the rear of the vehicle, where there are also two radiators, and a Ki-gas cold-weather starter is fitted. The Fox has the same fluid coupling, five speed pre-selecting epicyclic gearbox, and transfer box as the Ferret, giving the vehicle five forward gears and another five in reverse. It can ford to a depth of

1m/3ft 3in with no preparation. If the water is deeper, the flotation screen can be raised into position in just two minutes and then the vehicle becomes amphibious and is driven in the water by the wheels of the car. The Fox is fully air-transportable and three can be carried at once by a C130 Hercules transport aircraft. It can also be deployed by parachute. The vehicle is fitted with night-fighting and night-driving equipment, but no NBC system is installed.

The Fox was not a successful vehicle and did not remain in service for long. Its turrets were removed and fitted to the Scorpion and the FV 432.

RIGHT: **The smoke dischargers have been moved from the hull and on to the front of the turret. The turret has a large overhang and so the driver's hatch was designed to fold to the side. The flotation screen is attached around the side of the hull of this vehicle.**

### Fox Light Armoured Car

**Country:** UK
**Entered service:** 1973
**Crew:** 3
**Weight:** 6,120kg/6 tons
**Dimensions:** Length – 5.08m/16ft 8in
    Height – 2.2m/7ft 3in
    Width – 2.13m/7ft
**Armament:** Main – 30mm/1.18in RARDEN cannon,
    and coaxial 7.62mm/0.3in machine-gun
    Secondary – Small arms
**Armour:** Classified
**Powerplant:** Jaguar XK 4.2-litre 6-cylinder
    142kW/190hp petrol engine
**Performance:** Speed – Road 104kph/65mph;
    Water 5.2kph/3mph
    Range – 434km/270 miles

LEFT: **The large size of this vehicle can be seen from the crew member standing at the rear of the vehicle. The reloading crane can be seen under the missile launching rail. On the rear of the TEL are two stabilizers that have to be put in place before the missile can be elevated on its rail.**

# Frog-7 Battlefield Missile System

The Frog (Free Range Over Ground) missile system was designed and built to deliver nuclear warheads on to the battlefield, just like the American Honest John system. The first in the series was the Filin (Eagle Owl), which has the NATO codename Frog-1. This entered service in 1955 but was not seen by the Western allies until the Moscow November Parade in 1987. The launching vehicle for this system was the 2P4, which was based on the IS-2 heavy tank. Not very many of these rocket systems were deployed as the whole system was very large and unwieldy and the missile was powered by seven separate solid-fuel rockets which did not always fire at the same time, making it inherently unstable. The Frog-2 (NATO codename Mars), using the 2P2 modified PT-76 amphibious tank as its carrier, came into service in the same year as the

Frog-1, but only 25 of these vehicles were built and it was more of a propaganda tool than a useful battlefield system.

The Frog-3 used the Luna-1 (NATO codename Moon-1) rocket and appeared in 1957. This was the first true battlefield tactical missile system and was mounted on 2P16 vehicles, some 200 of these being produced for the Soviet Army and a further 100 for export. The vehicle was very similar to the 2P2 and was based on the PT-76 tank. It had a road speed of 44kph/27.3mph and could fire its first rocket within 15 minutes of parking, but reloading could take up to 60 minutes. The same vehicle was used for the Frog-3, Frog-4 and Frog-5 and remained in service for several years.

The final version of the Frog family was the Frog-7 which used the Luna-M rocket (NATO codename Moon-3) and the

RIGHT: **This is a reload vehicle for the Frog-7 system. The same chassis as the TEL is used, except that the crane and launching rail have been removed and replaced with three fixed transport ramps. The official designation of this vehicle was 9T29.**

LEFT: **This Frog-7 system is ready for firing. Behind the TEL on the road is a column of tanks. Each Frog battery consisted of four TEL vehicles and 170 personnel. Each battery carries seven missiles for each TEL.** ABOVE: **The cab of the TEL has its blast screen folded down on to the glacis of the vehicle. The engine compartment is mounted behind the cab of the vehicle. The crews for the two TEL vehicles are being briefed by their officer.**

9P113 TEL (Transporter, Erector and Launcher). This was based on the ZIL-135LM 8x8 heavy truck that was used for several rocket and transport duties. The ZIL-135LM was built at the Bryansk Automobile Plant near Moscow and was designated BAZ-135 but the Soviet Army still referred to the vehicle as the ZIL-135LM. The crew cab is at the front of the vehicle and holds four men. Before the missile is fired, an armoured cover which normally lies on the top of the front sub-nose of the vehicle is put in place by the crew to protect the windscreen from the rocket blast. Behind the cab is the engine bay. The engine area has two ZIL-135 8-cylinder petrol engines, with one engine for each side of the vehicle powering all four wheels on that side. Power steering was fitted on the front and rear axle and a central tyre pressure system was fitted as standard. Mounted behind the front axle and on the rear of the vehicle are four stabilizing jacks. In the middle of the vehicle are cable reels which are used for sending signals to the missile from a remote firing position some 25m/82ft away. On the right-hand side between the third and fourth axle is a 4,064kg/4-ton crane which is used for reloading. The hydraulically operated missile

erecting mechanism is at the rear of the vehicle, while the sighting and elevation controls are on the left-hand side. There is also a small platform that folds down to allow the operator to reach the sighting controls.

These vehicles were relatively cheap at just 25,000 US dollars when they came into service with the Soviet Army in 1965 and were the last unguided nuclear weapon in service with the Soviet Union and other Warsaw Pact members. The Bryansk plant produced 750 of these vehicles of which 380 have been exported and it is estimated that in 1999, Russia still had 1,450 nuclear warheads in stock for the Frog-7. The Frog has now been phased out of service with the Russian Army but is still in service with a number of Middle East countries.

The Luna-M missile is capable of carrying nuclear, high-explosive, chemical and sub munitions warheads. It has a minimum range of 15km/9.3 miles and a maximum of 65km/40.4 miles, but is not very accurate as it has a circular error of probability of between 500–700m/1,640–2,297ft, which means you could aim at an airfield and definitely hit it but not a target the size of a bridge.

ABOVE: **These vehicles are taking part in a victory parade. Between the first and second wheels is the forward stabilizer, one on each side of the vehicle. The reload crane can be clearly seen in this picture.**

## Frog-7 Missile System

**Country:** USSR
**Entered service:** 1965
**Crew:** 4
**Weight:** 20,411kg/20.1 tons
**Dimensions:** Length – 10.69m/35ft 1in
 Height – With missile 3.35m/11ft
 Width – 2.8m/9ft 2in
**Armament:** Main – 1 x Luna-M missile
 Secondary – Small arms
**Armour:** None
**Powerplant:** 2 x ZIL 135 8-cylinder 132kW/180hp
 petrol engine
**Performance:** Speed – 40kph/25mph
 Range – 650km/400 miles

# FV 432 Armoured Personnel Carrier

The first prototype for the FV 432 was completed in 1961, the first vehicle of this series being the earlier FV 431 which did not enter production as there was no need for an armoured load carrier. In 1962, GKN Sankey was given a contract to mass-produce the FV 432 or "Trojan" as it was called when it first entered service, but this name was dropped to avoid confusion with the Trojan car company. The first production vehicles were completed in 1963 and the FV 432 entered service with the British Army replacing the Humber "Pig" and Saracen APC over a period of time. The FV 432 was due to be replaced in the mid-1980s by the Warrior, but this has not happened due to defence cutbacks and the FV 432 is expected to remain in service for some years yet. These vehicles are currently undergoing a refurbishment programme to extend their service life.

The FV 432 is basically box-shaped and is an all-steel welded construction. The armour of the vehicle is proof against small arms fire and shell splinters. The driver sits in the front of the vehicle on the left-hand side and has a wide-angle periscope mounted in his hatch. The vehicle commander/gunner is situated behind the driver and has a cupola that can be rotated through 360 degrees with a mount for a single 7.62mm/0.3in GPMG mounted on the front of it. The driver's and commander's positions are open inside the vehicle and the commander can communicate with the driver by hitting him in

TOP: **This British FV 432 is on exercise in Germany. All the hatches on this vehicle are in the open position. The driver's and vehicle commander's positions are at the top of the picture. The large circular hatch above the crew compartment is in the open position, and a section of British troops are debussing.** ABOVE: **A side view of an FV 432 showing the exhaust system running the length of the vehicle. The exhaust stopped just by the rear exit, so at times when the vehicle was stopped, exhaust gases would enter the infantry compartment.**

the shoulders to indicate any desired changes of direction. Unfortunately this can be very painful after a while! Next to them on the right-hand side of the vehicle is the engine bay. Behind this is the infantry compartment which extends to the rear of the vehicle. This compartment can hold ten fully armed troops who sit on bench seats, five down each side of the vehicle facing each other. Above them is a large single circular hatch that is divided in the middle and, when opened, folds flush with the top of the vehicle on each side. Each half-hatch is hinged in the middle making opening easier. The bench seats can be folded up when not in use so the vehicle can then be used as a cargo carrier. At the rear of the vehicle is a single large door that opens outwards and to the right allowing the troops to debus very quickly, with the open rear door acting as a shield. The exhaust system is mounted on the left-hand side of the vehicle with the NBC system fitted to the right-hand side. All marks of the vehicle are fitted with a full NBC system.

The FV 432 was usually fitted with the Peak Engineering 7.62mm/0.3in turret, but the 30mm/1.18in turret from the Fox armoured car was mounted on a few vehicles of the Berlin Brigade. The turret was fitted behind the commander's position and into the upper hatch, which was now fixed in the closed position, and had a full 360-degree traverse, while behind the turret was a small circular hatch. The FV 432 is not amphibious but the Mk 1 was at first fitted with a flotation screen that could be raised in ten minutes, with the vehicle using its tracks to power it in the water. The flotation screen was not installed in the Mk 2 variant.

The FV 432 has been produced in three main marks. The Mk 1 was powered by a Rolls-Royce B81 8-cylinder 179kW/240hp petrol engine. The Mk 2 started to appear in 1966 and was fitted with a diesel engine that had a multi-fuel capability that

improved reliability and range. The last mark was the 2/1 and this had improvements to the exhaust system and the engine area. The vehicle commander is extremely vulnerable in the FV 432 and has no protection when manning the machine-gun with the hatch open. By 1967, many were slating the vehicle because it lacked heavy armament like that of the new Soviet BMP-1. However, no NATO APC could match the BMP for firepower.

ABOVE: **An FV 432 mine plough developed by the British Army but never seriously put into service. The glacis plate of the vehicle has several control boxes for the plough fitted to it. The plough blade is constructed in sections, so if one section is damaged it can be replaced quickly.** BELOW: **Another mine-clearing device fitted and tested on the FV 432 was the flail. The vehicle was called the Aardvark. The large box on the rear of the vehicle holds the lane-marking equipment. This device did not enter service with the British Army.**

MIDDLE LEFT: **The vehicle commander has a 7.62mm/0.3in machine-gun fitted to his cupola. The large boxes either side of the rear door are for storage. There**

was never enough storage space in or on the FV 432; many units fitted wire-mesh storage bins to the rear of the vehicle.
LEFT: **A 432 Mk 1 fitted with a RARDEN turret from the cancelled Fox armoured car. This vehicle is also fitted with a flotation screen around the top of the FV 432. On the front of the vehicle is a trim vane. The 432 is moved through the water by its tracks.**

### FV 432 Armoured Personnel Carrier

**Country:** UK
**Entered service:** 1963
**Crew:** 2 plus 10 infantry
**Weight:** 15,240kg/15.1 tons
**Dimensions:** Length – 5.25m/17ft 7in
  Height – 2.29m/7ft 6in
  Width – 2.8m/9ft 2in
**Armament:** Main – 7.62mm/0.3in General Purpose
  machine-gun
  Secondary – Small arms
**Armour:** Maximum – 12mm/0.47in
**Powerplant:** Rolls-Royce K60 No.4 Mk 4F
  6-cylinder 170kW/240hp diesel/multi-fuel engine
**Performance:** Speed – 52kph/32mph
  Range – 483km/300 miles

LEFT: **This German Gepard has the rear surveillance radar in the raised position. When the vehicle is moving, the surveillance radar folds back into the horizontal position. The vehicle commander is using a manual sight, attached to his cupola.** ABOVE: **Both radar dishes on this Gepard are in the raised active position. A bank of four smoke dischargers is fitted to each side of the bottom of the turret.**

# Gepard Self-Propelled Anti-Aircraft Gun

In 1961, contracts were issued to two companies for the development of a new Self-Propelled Anti-Aircraft Gun (SPAAG) for the *Bundeswehr* (German Army) as a replacement for the American M42. However, the whole project was cancelled in 1964 as the projected main chassis was considered to be too small and the tracking radar was not fully developed. In 1965, it was decided that a new all-weather design based on the Leopard 1 MBT chassis was required. Two development contracts were issued in 1966 for two vehicles armed with 3cm/1.18in guns and two vehicles armed with 3.5cm/1.38in guns. In 1970, following the decision to concentrate on the 3.5cm/1.38in vehicle, an order for 420 Gepards was placed, with the first vehicles entering service in 1976. The Belgian Army placed a contract for 55 Gepards that was fulfilled between 1977 and 1980, while the Dutch Army order for 95 vehicles was completed over the same period. In 1998 the German Government donated 43 Gepard vehicles to the Romanian Army along with training and maintenance equipment. The first of these were delivered in 1999.

The all-welded hull of the Gepard is slightly longer than the Leopard MBT while the armour on the vehicle has been reduced in thickness. The driver is located in the front of the vehicle on the right-hand side due to the tracking radar being mounted on the front of the turret. Next to the driver is the auxiliary power unit which is a Daimler-Benz OM314 70.8kW/ 95hp engine. The exhaust pipe for this runs along the left-hand side of the hull to the rear of the vehicle. The vehicle is fitted with a full NBC system.

The two-man turret is positioned in the middle of the vehicle; the commander is on the left with the gunner on the right and both are provided with their own hatch which is mounted in the roof of the turret. Both the gunner and commander have a fully

ABOVE: **On the front of the turret is the tracking radar. Targets are acquired by the surveillance radar and then the most prominent threat is worked out by computer and the target information passed to the tracking radar, which then locks the guns on to the target.**

stabilized panoramic telescope sight which is mounted on the roof of the turret and is used for optically tracking aerial targets and for use against ground targets. The optical sights can be linked to the radar and computer, and a Siemens laser rangefinder is also fitted for engaging ground targets. Mounted on the rear of the turret is the pulse-Doppler search radar, which has a 360-degree traverse, a range of 15km/9.3 miles, and an IFF (Identification Friend or Foe) capability. Once a target has been acquired the information is passed to the tracking radar which is mounted at the front of the turret between the guns. The computer and radar systems are capable of dealing with several targets at once. The main

armament is two Oerlikon 35mm/1.38in KDA cannon. Each gun barrel has a firing rate of 550 rounds per minute and the vehicle carries 660 rounds in total, with 310 anti-aircraft shells and 20 rounds of armour-piercing ammunition for each barrel. A normal burst of fire lasts for a fraction of a second and can be up to a maximum of 40 rounds. The guns normally open fire when the target is at a distance of between 3,000m/9,842ft and 4,000m/13,123ft with the rounds reaching the target at a range of between 2,000m/6,561ft and 3,000m/9,842ft, the computer calculating the predicted position of the target. The guns are mounted externally on the sides of the turret with the ammunition being fed in on hermetically sealed chutes, which keeps the gun fumes away from the crew.

In 1996, the vehicle systems were upgraded so that the Gepard could remain in service for several more years. The Germans upgraded 147 of their vehicles while the Dutch upgraded 60, the main improvements being to the fire-control systems and the ammunition. As part of this project, the

ABOVE LEFT: **This is a Dutch Gepard. The Dutch fitted different surveillance radar to that installed by the Germans; it is shaped like a large letter "T" which rotates at 60 revolutions per minute. The Dutch also fitted banks of six smoke dischargers to each side of the bottom of the turret.** ABOVE: **The barrels of this Gepard have been covered in camouflage netting. The turret can complete a full rotation of 360 degrees in just 4 seconds. The fumes from the gun barrels and the empty cases are ejected directly to the outside of the vehicle.**

German and Dutch vehicles were data-linked so they can exchange information. The upgrade programme was finished in 2002 and should keep the vehicle in service until 2015. The German upgraded version is known as the Gepard Flakpanzer 1A2 while the Dutch vehicle is now known as the PRTL 35mm GWI. Since 1999, Krauss-Maffei Wegmann, who produced the upgrade package, have developed another upgrade which involves the fitting of four "fire and forget" Stinger SAMs, two being mounted externally on each 35mm/1.38in gun mount. This is not yet operational.

LEFT: **This Gepard is in travelling mode. The tracking radar dish has been folded forward to protect the dish from damage. With the surveillance radar folded down, the height of the vehicle is lowered by 1m/39in. Acquisition speed of the radar is 56 degrees per second, with a full traverse of the turret taking just four seconds.**

## Gepard SPAAG

**Country:** West Germany
**Entered service:** 1976
**Crew:** 3
**Weight:** 45,009kg/44.3 tons
**Dimensions:** Length – 7.68m/25ft 2in
　　　　　Height – 3.01m/9ft 9in to top of turret
　　　　　Width – 3.27m/10ft 7in
**Armament:** Main – 2 x 35mm/1.38in Oerlikon
　　　　　KDA guns
　　　　　Secondary – None
**Armour:** Maximum – 70mm/2.76in
**Powerplant:** MTU MB 838 Ca M500 10-cylinder
　　　　　619kW/830hp multi-fuel engine
**Performance:** Speed – 64kph/40.5mph
　　　　　Range – 550km/340 miles

LEFT: **The vehicle is fitted with three stabilizing jacks. One is mounted in front of the rear wheels on each side of the vehicle and a single jack is mounted at the rear of the vehicle in the centre.**
ABOVE: **A British Honest John during a live-firing exercise. The missile could be fitted with two 20 or 40 kiloton W31 nuclear warheads. It could also be fitted with a 680kg/1,500lb high-explosive or 564kg/1,243lb chemical warhead.**

# Honest John Missile System

Development of the M31 started at Redstone Arsenal, USA, in May 1950. The Douglas Aircraft Company was appointed to assist with development and later to carry out production, the first production contract being for 2,000 rockets. The M31 was deployed in Europe in June 1954 and it remained in service until 1961 when the improved M50 Honest John, which was lighter and had an increased range, replaced it. In July 1982, the Honest John system was declared obsolete as the Lance nuclear system came into service.

The rocket was a solid-fuel system and therefore required no countdown time and could remain in storage for several years with no maintenance. The M31 had a maximum range of 19.3km/12 miles, which meant that when firing a 20-kilotonne/19,684-ton nuclear warhead the fallout area would have been greater than the range of the missile, whereas the M50 missile, with its range of 48.3km/30 miles, would have been safer for the crew to use. The missile was unguided and required the whole vehicle to be pointed at the target area. The missile could be fitted with either a conventional high-explosive or a nuclear warhead and was never used in action.

The Transporter, Erector and Launcher (TEL) was built by the International Harvester Company and used the M139 5,080kg/5-ton truck, a stretched version of the M54 5,080kg/5-ton truck, as the base vehicle for the conversion. The TEL was designated M289 and was a 6x6 configuration which gave it excellent cross-country ability. The vehicle had the engine located at the front, the three-man soft-top crew cab behind it and the missile erector at the rear. The first version of the TEL had an "A" frame supporting the launch rail and this was pivoted in the middle of the vehicle above the two centrally mounted stabilizers while the launch rail protruded over the front of the TEL by 1.8m/6ft, restricting the driver's vision. The improved TEL had a much shorter launch rail, the front of which could be folded back on itself while travelling. The elevation controls were at the rear of the vehicle on the left-hand side.

ABOVE: **A control wire is run from the vehicle to a command position a safe distance away from the back-blast of the missile. The three-man crew of this vehicle are getting instructions from an officer before firing the missile.**

## M289 TEL

**Country:** USA
**Entered service:** 1954
**Crew:** 3
**Weight:** 16,400kg/16.1 tons
**Dimensions:** Length – 9.89m/32ft 5in
  Height – 2.9m/9ft 5in
  Width – 2.67m/8ft 8in
**Armament:** Main – M31 Honest John Missile
  Secondary – Small arms
**Armour:** None
**Powerplant:** Continental R6602 6-cylinder
  146kW/196hp petrol engine
**Performance:** Speed – 90kph/56mph
  Range – 480km/300 miles

LEFT: **The launching arm on this vehicle is retracted for travelling and the driver's and vehicle commander/gunner's hatches are in the open position. Above the gunner's position is a domed armoured sight.** ABOVE: **The launching arm of this Hornet is in the raised firing position. This vehicle and missile system was specifically designed to be dropped by parachute.**

# Hornet Malkara Anti-Tank Missile System

The Hornet was developed from the Humber "Pig" 1-ton APC, and was originally designed to give the armoured divisions of the British Army a long-range anti-tank capability. This was intended to replace the Conqueror heavy tank with a guided missile system as it was felt that the tank no longer had a role on the modern battlefield.

The Hornet was based on the Humber 1,016kg/1-ton 4x4 vehicle and while it used the same chassis and engine as the standard vehicle, the crew compartment and the rear of the vehicle were modified to take the Malkara wire-guided missile system. The engine was located at the front, with the crew compartment behind and the missile launching arm fitted to the rear of the vehicle. The crew compartment was configured with the

driver on the right, the commander/gunner on the left and the radio operator in the middle. The driver and radio operator also doubled as reload crew for the vehicle.

The superstructure at the rear of the 1,016kg/1-ton APC vehicle was removed and replaced by two storage boxes for two Malkara missiles and the launcher hydraulic arm. When travelling the launching arm was stowed in a lowered position below the top of the crew compartment. When the vehicle reached its firing location it halted and the launching arm was raised to the firing position, some 90cm/3ft above the crew compartment, so that the missiles had a clear flight to the target. The commander/gunner had an optical sight that was mounted in the roof of the crew

compartment and controlled the missile using a joystick. Each missile had two flares attached at the rear which helped the gunner to track it to the target. The missile weighed 91kg/200lb of which the warhead was 27kg/60lb; this represented the largest warhead carried by any anti-tank missile at the time.

The Malkara missile was a joint British and Australian development, but was never very successful and the Hornet Malkara was replaced in service with the British Army from 1965 onwards by the Ferret Mk 2/6 armed with Vigilant ATGW missiles. The Hornet could rightly be described as a very expensive white elephant when compared with the economic Ferret.

LEFT: **The rear storage area of the Hornet, where two reload missiles are carried. The rear hatch splits in two with the bottom part folding downwards to form a shelf, while the top half of the hatch folds flat on the top of the storage box. The wings are stored separately from the missiles in the rear of the vehicle.**

## Hornet Malkara ATGM

**Country:** UK
**Entered service:** 1958
**Crew:** 3
**Weight:** 5,893kg/5.8 tons
**Dimensions:** Length – 5.05m/16ft 7in
　　Height – 2.34m/7ft 8in
　　Width – 2.22m/7ft 3in
**Armament:** Main – 4 x Malkara ATGM
　　Secondary – 7.62mm/0.3in General Purpose
　　machine-gun
**Armour:** Maximum – 10mm/0.394in
**Powerplant:** Rolls-Royce B60 Mk 5A 6-cylinder
　　89kW/120hp petrol engine
**Performance:** Speed – 64kph/40mph
　　Range – 402km/250 miles

LEFT: **This Humber Pig is fitted with a grill for pushing road blocks such as burning cars out of the way of the vehicle. An armoured plate has been fitted to the rear of the vehicle to stop fire-bombs or other objects being thrown under the vehicle.**
ABOVE: **The inside of the vehicle commander's door. Mounted in the door is an armoured vision port. The clear plastic tank in front of the commander's position is a screen-wash bottle. The bottle is filled with a chemical that can remove paint and other liquid that might be thrown at the vehicle.**

# Humber "Pig" 1-Ton Armoured Personnel Carrier

In the late 1940s and early 1950s, the Humber/Rootes Group developed a range of 1,016kg/1-ton armoured vehicles for the British Army. The Saracen APC was also under development at the same time but production proved to be slow and so the Humber "Pig" APC was developed as an interim solution. It was designed as a battlefield taxi and not as a combat vehicle; troops would debus away from the action and attack on foot. This interim vehicle entered production in 1954 and came into service in 1955. It was originally intended to produce only a few vehicles but the total quickly mounted to 1,700. This vehicle was so successful and adaptable that it is still in service with the British Army in 2005.

Humber took the basic 1,016kg/1-ton 4x4 cargo vehicle and added an armoured roof and rear doors to make a very basic APC for the army. The exact derivation of the vehicle's label

"Pig" is not known for certain, but it is certainly difficult to drive and lives up to its name.

The Pig is an all-welded construction with the engine at the front and the crew compartment behind. The driver and vehicle commander sit side by side in the front of the crew compartment behind the engine. Each of them has a windscreen to their front that can be covered when in action by an armoured shutter that folds down from the roof of the vehicle. Both also have an access door in the side of the vehicle and above them in the roof are two circular hatches. There are two firing ports in each side of the crew compartment with a further two mounted in the rear doors of the vehicle.

In the early 1960s it was thought that there were enough Saracen APCs in service and as the FV 432 was also just coming into service, it was decided to sell off the now-redundant Pigs. However, when the "Troubles" started in Northern Ireland in 1969, the army was asked to step in to help the police in maintaining the peace. The Pig was chosen to give the troops some mobility and protection without further arousing passions in a situation of civil unrest, being relatively small and innocuous and not having the aggressive appearance of a tank. Unfortunately, only a few of these vehicles had been kept in reserve, the majority having been scrapped or sold off to private collectors and the Belgian armed forces. These were bought back at an inflated price

LEFT: **The driver's position inside the Humber Pig. The gear stick is between the seats with the handbrake next to the driver's seat. The dashboard is in the centre of the vehicle so both the driver and commander can see it.**

LEFT: **This Humber Pig has been fitted with a six-barrel smoke and CS gas discharger. Under the rear of the vehicle, the armoured plate to stop bombs being thrown under the vehicle can be clearly seen.**
BELOW: **The inside of a Humber Pig command vehicle. One set of seats has been removed and replaced with a map table. Two wooden boards separate the driver and vehicle commander's cab from the troop compartment of the vehicle. The rear doors of the vehicle are held open by a simple metal hook and eye.**

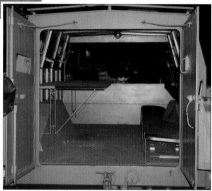

and refurbished, and some 500 Pigs were sent to Northern Ireland. In 1972 it was discovered that the IRA had acquired armour-piercing ammunition that could damage the vehicle and cause casualties inside. As a result, Operation "Bracelet" was launched to upgrade the armour of the Pig and fit vision blocks to the open firing ports. The vehicle's suspension was also strengthened to accommodate the additional weight, and an extra armoured shutter was added to the rear of the vehicle which would fall into place when the rear doors were opened, protecting the legs of the men following the vehicle.

When the Saracen was withdrawn from Northern Ireland in 1984 the Pig had to take over its role and this led to a number of specialist conversions with exotic sounding names. The "Kremlin Pig" was covered with wire mesh as a protection against the Soviet RPG-7 rocket launcher. The "Flying Pig" has large side-mounted riot screens fitted to the vehicle. These fold back along the length of the crew compartment when not in use, but when in the open position have the appearance of wings and give troops protection from stones or other objects thrown at them. The "Holy Pig" has a Plexiglas fixed observation turret in the roof, the front of which can be folded down. Other Pig variants had smoke and CS gas launchers placed in the roof which can be fired from inside the vehicle, and large bull-bar bumpers have been fitted to the front.

The Pig proved to be a very reliable and "squaddy-proof" AFV especially given the "interim" nature of the design, and it continues to be an extremely valuable vehicle. The Saxon has replaced the Humber Pig in many roles.

ABOVE: **This is a "Flying Pig" in operation in Northern Ireland during the "Troubles" of the 1970s. The wire-mesh screens looked like a set of wings when deployed. Behind the wings of the vehicle are British troops. The soldier in the front is firing a baton-round gun, which could discharge either CS gas or rubber bullets.**

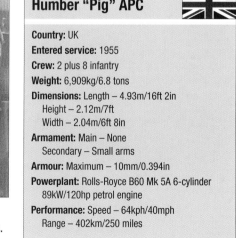

## Humber "Pig" APC

**Country:** UK
**Entered service:** 1955
**Crew:** 2 plus 8 infantry
**Weight:** 6,909kg/6.8 tons
**Dimensions:** Length – 4.93m/16ft 2in
   Height – 2.12m/7ft
   Width – 2.04m/6ft 8in
**Armament:** Main – None
   Secondary – Small arms
**Armour:** Maximum – 10mm/0.394in
**Powerplant:** Rolls-Royce B60 Mk 5A 6-cylinder 89kW/120hp petrol engine
**Performance:** Speed – 64kph/40mph
   Range – 402km/250 miles

LEFT: **This HUMVEE has been fitted with an extended exhaust system, which allows the vehicle to wade through 1m/39in of water. The bonnet of the vehicle tilts forward to give access to the engine.**
ABOVE: **The driver's position is on the left with the vehicle commander on the right. The large console in the middle of the vehicle has the communications equipment mounted in it. When the vehicle is fitted with a roof-mounted machine-gun, the turret gunner stands between the rear seats.**

# Hummer Multi-Role Vehicle

Development of the High Mobility Multipurpose Wheeled Vehicle (HMMWV or HUMVEE) started in the 1970s. In 1983, the American armed forces signed a 1.2 billion-dollar production contract with the AM General Corporation under which AM General would produce 55,000 of these new vehicles for them between 1984 and 1989. Better known to the troops who use the vehicle as the "Hummer", it was given the official designation of M998. A further option was exercised by the US military for an additional 15,000 vehicles, while in 1989 another order was placed for 33,000 vehicles. More orders have since been placed for uparmoured variants, as a result of combat experience, which will bring the total production run to 125,000 vehicles so far.

The basic HMMWV has the engine in the front of the vehicle, the crew compartment in the middle and a load-carrying area in the rear. The vehicle is permanently in the 4x4 configuration and the bonnet tilts forward to allow easy access to the air-cooled 6.2-litre diesel engine. The crew compartment has a box frame steel roll-cage fitted to it, while the rest of the body is made from aluminium that is riveted and glued into position. This makes the replacement of damaged panels easier and quicker than if it were an all-welded construction. The four-man crew sit either side of the power transfer, two in the front and two in the rear of the compartment. There is a hatch in the roof above the crew compartment when the vehicle is fitted with a machine-gun or other weapon

system. The HMMWV can be fitted with a wide selection of armament ranging from a basic 7.62mm/0.3in machine-gun to a 30mm/1.18in cannon, Hellfire ATGMs or Starstreak AAGMs.

The HMMWV has been built in 18 different variations and development has continued with many improvements based on the results of combat reports. The engine has also been improved several times since coming into service. The original engine developed 97kW/130hp but this has now increased to 142kW/190hp. The latest version of the vehicle, designated the M1114, has increased armour and most HMMWVs will be brought up to this standard.

LEFT: **The front of the HUMVEE, with the recessed lights and a cow-catcher on the front of the vehicle. Increased cooling is supplied to the engine from the grill in the bonnet. The vehicle now carries the official American designation of M998.**

## HMMWV M1114

**Country:** USA
**Entered service:** 1985
**Crew:** 1 plus 3 infantry
**Weight:** 5,489kg/5.4 tons
**Dimensions:** Length – 4.99m/16ft 4in
   Height – 1.9m/6ft 3in
   Width – 2.3m/7ft 7in
**Armament:** Main – 1 x 7.62mm/0.3in
   GP machine-gun (basic variant)
   Secondary – Small arms
**Armour:** Classified
**Powerplant:** General Motors 6.5-litre 8-cylinder
   142kW/190hp diesel engine
**Performance:** Speed – 125kph/78mph
   Range – 443km/275 miles

LEFT: **A trio of long wheelbase reconnaissance Land Rover Defenders. The vehicles have been fitted with several heavy machine-guns, and smoke dischargers have been fixed to the top of the front bumper of the vehicle. The vehicles are all covered in extra equipment.** ABOVE: **The inside of "Dinky", the short wheelbase Land Rover Defender developed for the British Army. The vehicle is fitted with a roll-bar to protect the crew if the vehicle turns over. In the rear of the vehicle is a pintle mount for a machine-gun or MILAN AT missile system.**

# Land Rover Defender Multi-Role Vehicles

The Land Rover has been in service with the British Army for over 45 years and has gone through many changes and improvements in that time. The latest series in service is the Defender which is produced in three chassis variations: 2.29m/90in, 2.79m/110in and 3.3m/130in. This is the distance between the wheel centres of the vehicle, known as the wheelbase. The Land Rover 90 and 110 are the core vehicles with the 130 being a special conversion vehicle, for example in the ambulance role. Development of the Defender started in 1983 when the then current range of Land Rover vehicles was beginning to show its age and in need of updating with modern technology. At first an order was placed for 950 of all types, followed by an order for 500 of the 90 version and 1,200 of the 110 version.

The Land Rover Defender uses the chassis and coil-spring suspension of the Range Rover and so is a stronger and more comfortable vehicle than the previous series of vehicles. In appearance, it is similar to other earlier models except that there are bulges over the wheel arches and there is a revised radiator grill. The windscreen is a one-piece unit and the vehicle is fitted with permanent four-wheel drive. The Defender is normally fitted with a diesel engine but an 8-cylinder petrol engine is also available. The roof is constructed from roll-bars and the gun-mounting. The weapons fit of the vehicle is very varied, but the basic configuration is three 7.62mm/0.3in GPMGs, one fitted in the front for use by the vehicle commander and two on a twin mount in the roof of the rear area. Other weapons available are a 30mm/1.18in cannon, TOW missiles, LAW 80 ATM or Browning 12.7mm/0.5in heavy machine-guns.

The Defender is available as a Special Operations Vehicle (SOV) and has been developed for the British SAS forces and the US Rangers. These vehicles are fitted with the 300Tdi direct injection intercooled diesel engine. The SOV is fully air-portable by heavy-lift aircraft such as the C-130 or can be under-slung from helicopters such as the Puma and Chinook.

ABOVE: **The famous SAS "Pink Panther"; this is a long wheelbase Land Rover. The vehicle has been fitted with several machine-guns and has smoke dischargers fixed to the top of the bodywork on the rear of the vehicle.**

## Land Rover Defender 110 SOV

**Country:** UK
**Entered service:** 1990
**Crew:** 1 plus up to 5 infantry
**Weight:** 3,050kg/3 tons
**Dimensions:** Length – 4.67m/15ft 4in
　　Height – 2.04m/6ft 8in
　　Width – 1.79m/5ft 10in
**Armament:** Main – 3 x 7.62mm/0.3in GPMGs
　　Secondary – Small arms
**Armour:** None
**Powerplant:** Rover 300Tdi 8-cylinder
　　100kW/134hp diesel engine
**Performance:** Speed – 90kph/56mph
　　Range – 450km/280 miles

LEFT: **The LAV-25 is a copy of the Swiss MOWAG Piranha. MOWAG was bought by General Motors of Canada. This vehicle is becoming the world's most successful armoured personnel carrier. This LAV-25 is in the basic setup and is armed with the M242 chain gun and two clusters of four smoke dischargers on the front of the turret.**

# LAV-25 Light Armoured Vehicles

In September 1981 the Diesel Division of General Motors Defence, who also own MOWAG of Switzerland, was awarded a 3.1 million-dollar contract to build four 8x8 Piranha vehicles for a selection competition to provide a new Light Armoured Vehicle (LAV) for the US Marine Corps and the US Army. The first two vehicles were delivered in October 1981. One was fitted with an Arrowpointe two-man turret armed with a 25mm/0.98in chain gun, while the other vehicle had the same turret armed with a 90mm/3.54in Cockerill Mk III gun. Both turrets had an M240 coaxial machine-gun and eight smoke dischargers fitted as standard. In September 1982, the Diesel Division won the LAV competition and while the originally planned contract for 969 vehicles was not signed, annual orders were placed for the vehicle. The US Army pulled out of the programme in 1984 but 758 vehicles had been built for the US Marine Corps by 1985. The first production LAV-25 vehicles, similar to the 8x8 Piranha, were delivered in 1983 and the last one in 1987.

The all-welded steel hull of the LAV-25 protects the crew from small-arms fire and shell splinters. The driver sits in the front of the vehicle on the left-hand side, next to the engine which is on the right with the air-inlet and outlet louvers on the hull top. The exhaust outlet is mounted on the right-hand side of the vehicle. In the middle of the vehicle is the two-man turret and the infantry compartment is in the rear of the vehicle. Access to the rear compartment is by two doors that open outwards, each of which has a vision port fitted. The troop compartment is connected to a centralized NBC system, but the six men that sit in this area, three down each side facing

ABOVE: **A LAV-25 armoured ambulance. This is a development of the logistics vehicle, which can be seen behind the ambulance. The ambulance is fitted with two clusters of four smoke dischargers on the rear roof of the vehicle.**

inwards, are very cramped. Above the compartment are two hatches that can give access to the outside and there is also an escape hatch in the body of the vehicle. The Delco two-man turret has the commander on the right and the gunner on the left and is fitted with an M242 25mm/0.98in McDonnell Douglas Helicopter Company chain gun as the main armament. The vehicle commander can also have a 7.62mm/0.3in M240 machine-gun fitted on a pintle mount in front of the turret hatch, and on each side of the turret front are four smoke dischargers. The turret is fitted with laser range-finding and a full range of night-fighting optics. The driver also has night-driving optics fitted. When the vehicle is travelling cross-country full eight-wheel drive can be engaged, but in less demanding situations the vehicle is driven in the more economic mode which supplies power only to the rear four wheels. The steering controls the front four wheels, and the vehicle is fully amphibious. The LAV-25 is fitted with two propellers that propel the vehicle when in the water and steering is achieved using four rudders. A trim vane is fitted to the front of the vehicle and it takes just three minutes to make the LAV ready for the water.

The LAV has been built in a number of variants. The LAV Logistics Vehicle has a crew of two, a higher roof and a crane is fitted to the vehicle. The LAV Mortar Carrier has a crew of five, with the mortar fitted in the middle of the vehicle on a turntable where the turret would normally be. A large double-folding hatch covers the space left by the turret opening. The LAV-ARV has a crew of five and has a boom with a 265-degree traverse. An "A"-frame support is fitted to be used when lifting heavy loads. The LAV Anti-Tank Vehicle mounts a twin TOW launcher that can traverse through 360 degrees. Fourteen reload missiles are carried in the vehicle. The last version to enter service was the LAV Air Defence System, which is fitted with the General Electric Blazer system. This has two four-round Stinger missile pods on the side of a turret that is also fitted with the GAU-12/U 25mm/0.98in Gatling gun.

These vehicles have proved to very reliable in service, but suffer from lack of internal personal equipment storage space for the crew.

ABOVE: **This LAV-25 is fitted with an Emerson twin TOW AT missile launcher. Two missiles are carried in the launcher, with a further 14 reloads carried inside the vehicle. This vehicle has a crew of three. The twin rear doors can be clearly seen in this picture.**

ABOVE: **A column of LAV-25 vehicles of the US Marine Corps in the Middle East. The large exhaust system on the side of the vehicle can be clearly seen. The front four wheels are used to steer the vehicle. These vehicles are not in a combat zone as they have no personal equipment stored on the outside.**

ABOVE: **This shows how cramped the command vehicle is when all the communication equipment is fitted. The vehicle has a crew of two but can carry five HQ staff in the rear.**

LEFT: **This mobile AA system was developed for the US Air Force. The one-man turret was armed with a 30mm/1.18in Gatling gun and four Stinger missiles. The project was dropped when the US Army took over airfield defence.**

### LAV-25 Light Armoured Vehicle 🍁

**Country:** Canada
**Entered service:** 1982
**Crew:** 3 plus 6 infantry
**Weight:** 12,792kg/12.6 tons
**Dimensions:** Length – 6.39m/21ft
　　　　　Height – 2.69m/8ft 8in
　　　　　Width – 2.5m/8ft 2in
**Armament:** Main – M242 25mm/0.98in chain gun, and coaxial M240 7.62mm/0.3in machine-gun
　　　　　Secondary – Pintle mounted M240 7.62mm/0.3in machine-gun
**Armour:** Maximum – 10mm/0.394in (estimated)
**Powerplant:** Detroit 6V-53T 6-cylinder 205kW/275hp diesel engine
**Performance:** Speed – Road 100kph/62mph; Water 10kph/6mph
　　　　　Range – 668km/415 miles

# LVTP-7 Armoured Amphibious Assault Vehicle

ABOVE: **An LVTP-7 on a training exercise. The driver can be seen with his head just out of his cupola. Behind him is an instructor squatting next to the vehicle commander's cupola. The vehicle commander and gunner are beside the gun turret.**

The standard LVT of the US Marine Corps post World War II was the LVTP-5A1. This was an unsatisfactory vehicle as it had a very limited land and water range, was unreliable, and difficult to maintain. In 1964, the Marine Corps issued a requirement for a new LVTP and a development contract was awarded to the FMC Corporation. Development started in 1966 and the final 15 vehicles commissioned were delivered in 1967. Trials were completed in 1969 and in June 1970 a contract was signed with FMC to supply 942 LVTP-7 (Landing Vehicle Tracked Personnel Model 7). The first vehicles were delivered to the Marine Corps in August 1971 with the first unit being equipped in March 1972 and the final deliveries to the Marines being made in 1974.

The all-welded aluminium hull gives the crew protection from small-arms fire and shell splinters. The engine is in the front of the vehicle and is placed on the centreline. The driver's position is alongside the engine on the right-hand side and is fitted with all-round vision blocks. Behind the driver on the left-hand side is the vehicle commander's position which is also fitted with all-round vision blocks while a periscope in the front of the commander's cupola allows him to see over the driver's position. The turret is on the right-hand side of the vehicle beside the engine. The gunner has all-round vision from nine vision blocks fitted into the cupola and the turret is armed with a 12.7mm/0.5in M85 machine-gun with two rates of fire: either 1,050 or 480 rounds per minute. The vehicle carries 1,000 rounds of ammunition for this weapon. The turret traverse mechanism is electro-hydraulic and has a full 360-degree traverse in under five seconds.

The LVTP has no NBC system, but is fitted with infrared night-driving lights. The suspension consists of six dual rubber-shod road wheels on each side and the track is single pin type, fitted with replaceable rubber pads. The main troop compartment is situated behind the turret and extends to the rear of the vehicle providing accommodation for 25 men. There

LEFT: **This LVTP-7 is moving at speed in deep snow. The boat-shaped hull can be clearly seen along with the long track length, which gives the vehicle a low ground pressure.**

are three bench seats in the rear: one down each side and one in the middle, each seating eight men, while the other seating position is available behind the vehicle commander's position. The centre bench seat can be removed and stored on the left-hand side of the compartment and the other two bench seats can be folded up so the vehicle can be used for moving supplies or wounded.

The LVTP is fully amphibious and requires no preparation time when entering the water. It is propelled by two water jets mounted on the rear of the vehicle in the sponsons, each jet having a hinged water deflector fitted at the rear which acts as a protective cover when not in use. The tracks of the vehicle can also be used to provide additional propulsion when the vehicle is in the water. The Marines enter and leave the vehicle by a power-operated ramp. In the left-hand side of the ramp there is a small access door, and above the troop compartment two very large spring-balanced hatches are installed. These are used for loading the vehicle when it is waterborne while taking on supplies alongside a ship.

In March 1977, FMC was awarded a contract for the conversion of 14 LVTPs to a new configuration known as the LVTP-7A1. This upgrade included an improved engine, better night-driving equipment and fighting optics, improved radios, an improved fire-suppression system, better troop compartment ventilation, improved weapon stations and an ability to generate smoke. Subsequently, the Marine Corps decided to upgrade all of their LVTP-7 vehicles to the new

standard in 1982, and this was completed by 1986. These vehicles have also been fitted with a new turret that has an additional 40mm/1.58in grenade launcher installed along with the 12.7mm/0.3in machine-gun. RAFAEL appliqué armour has also been fitted to a large number of the new LVTP-7A1 vehicles since 1987. These vehicles are expected to remain in service for several more years as a result of this service life extension programme. They are currently operational in Iraq.

ABOVE: **A column of LVTP-7 vehicles moving through the surf on the soft sand of a beach. The three-man crew are in their crew positions in the vehicle. The lights on the front of the vehicle are recessed into the hull to help protect them.** LEFT: **The three crew cupolas can be clearly seen. The driver's position is in the front on the left with the commander's behind. On the right of the vehicle is the gunner's turret.**

### LVTP-7A1 Armoured Amphibious Assault Vehicle

**Country:** USA
**Entered service:** 1977
**Crew:** 3 plus 25 infantry
**Weight:** 23,936kg/23.6 tons
**Dimensions:** Length – 7.94m/26ft 1in
Height – 3.26m/10ft 8in
Width – 3.27m/10ft 9in
**Armament:** Main – 12.7mm/0.5in M2 HB machine-gun, and 40mm/1.58in grenade launcher
Secondary – Small arms
**Armour:** Maximum – 45mm/1.77in
**Powerplant:** Cummins VT400 8-cylinder 298kW/400hp turbocharged diesel engine
**Performance:** Speed – Road 72kph/45mph;
Water 13kph/8mph
Range – 482km/300 miles

RIGHT: **The LVTP-7 has been in service for over 30 years. A new vehicle is required for the US Marines, and the AAAV is being developed by General Dynamics to fill this role. The first of the development vehicles were due out in 2004, but this has now been deferred for financial reasons.**

# M42 Duster Self-Propelled Anti-Aircraft Gun

In August 1951, the US Army authorized the development of a replacement vehicle for the M19A1 SPAAG and initially an interim design called the T-141 was developed. The final design was to be the T-141A1, and a fire control vehicle, the T-53, was also going to be developed but both were cancelled in 1952. However, the T-141 put into production and standardized as the M42. The first vehicle was produced in April 1952, with the last vehicle being handed over to the Army in December 1953. Total production was 3,700 vehicles.

The M42 used many of the same automotive components as the M41 light tank. The driver and radio operator/commander sat side by side in the front of the vehicle with the driver on the left. Behind them was the gun turret which was armed with twin 40mm/1.58in M2A1 cannon and had a crew of four, two gunners and two loaders. The turret had a power traverse and could complete a full 360-degree traverse in nine seconds. The guns could be fired in single shot or fully automatic modes and could discharge 120 rounds per minute when in the latter. When engaging ground targets the vehicle had a maximum range of 3,000m/9,842ft and a maximum ceiling of 3,962m/13,000ft. The Duster could carry 480 rounds of 40mm/1.58in ammunition in bins around the inside of the turret, which had a 7.62mm/0.3in machine-gun mount on the right-hand side. The engine and transmission was

in the rear of the vehicle and there were only had three gears – two forward and one reverse. The suspension was a torsion-bar type supporting five road wheels per side. The M42 had no NBC system and was not capable of any deep fording, but was fitted with infrared night-driving lights.

The Duster had a new engine fitted in 1956 which gave the vehicle an increased range and was redesignated the M42A1. The turrets of both vehicles could be manually operated and could track aircraft at up to 966kph/600mph, but they could only be used effectively during daylight.

TOP: **The chassis of the Walker Bulldog M41 light tank was used for the development of this vehicle. The gun turret was very open and so gave the gun crew no protection.** ABOVE: **A column of American armoured vehicles being led by two M42 Dusters in the early 1950s. The driver and co-driver are in their positions in the front of the M42, while the rest of the gun crew are riding on the open gun turret.**

LEFT: **Two American M42 Dusters with a crewman standing between them. The small size of the vehicle can be seen by the size of the crewman. Some of the vehicles were improved upon by fitting anti-grenade screens to the top of the turret.**

## M42 Duster SPAAG

**Country:** USA
**Entered service:** 1952
**Crew:** 6
**Weight:** 22,452kg/22.1 tons
**Dimensions:** Length – 6.36m/19ft 5in
    Height – 2.85m/9ft 4in
    Width – 3.22m/10ft 7in
**Armament:** Main – 2 x 40mm/1.58in M2A1 cannon
    Secondary – 7.62mm/0.3in machine-gun
**Armour:** Maximum – 25mm/0.98in
**Powerplant:** Continental or Lycoming 6-cylinder 373kW/500hp petrol engine
**Performance:** Speed – 72kph/45mph
    Range – 160km/100 miles

LEFT: **The lowered idler wheel, which is now on the same level as the road wheels, is clear from this profile. The short barrel length is also clearly shown; it does not overhang the front of the vehicle.**
ABOVE: **This M44 has been fitted with a canvas roof which gives the crew some protection from the weather. The exhaust system is located on the right-hand side of the vehicle. The engine is mounted in the front of the vehicle, hence all the engine intake grills on the glacis.**

# M44 155mm Self-Propelled Gun

Development of this vehicle started in 1947 and two prototypes, given the designation T99, were built. The vehicle was to utilize as many automotive parts from the M41 light tank as possible to make maintenance and sourcing spare parts easier to manage. The vehicle was redesignated the T99E1 and a contract was issued in 1952 when production started. A number of changes were required due to problems with the pilot models, but by the time these had been finalized 250 of the production vehicles had been built. The new improved vehicle, now called the T194, was standardized in September 1953 as the M44, and all the service vehicles already produced were upgraded to the new T194 standard.

The hull of the M44 was an all-welded steel construction, with the engine and transmission in the front of the vehicle. The transmission was a General Motors Model CD-500-3 cross-drive unit which gave the vehicle two forward gears and one reverse. The suspension was a torsion-bar system and the rear idler was lowered to form a sixth road wheel. The crew compartment was mounted high up on the vehicle and included the vehicle driver who was positioned at the front on the right-hand side. The crew compartment was open-topped but could have a canvas cover fitted to protect the crew from the weather. The gun was an M45 howitzer which was installed on an M80 mount, while a close-defence 12.7mm/0.3in machine-gun was

fitted to the left-hand side of the vehicle behind the driver. At the rear of the vehicle a recoil spade was fitted and when this was lowered into position a platform could be folded down from the rear of the vehicle. This allowed the twin rear doors, which serve as ammunition storage, to open. The exhaust system was fitted to the top of the front track guards and was the source of a major problem as engine fumes travelled back into the crew compartment, gassing the crew.

The M44 later received an improved engine giving greater range and fuel economy and this new vehicle was standardized in 1956 as the M44A1. The British Army also used the M44.

LEFT: **The driver's position was located in the turret of the vehicle on the left-hand side. In front of his position was a small windscreen, while behind the driver was the close-support machine-gun. A model with overhead armour was built and trialled, but was not adopted for service by any country.**

## M44 155mm SPG

**Country:** USA
**Entered service:** 1953
**Crew:** 5
**Weight:** 28,346kg/27.9 tons
**Dimensions:** Length – 6.16m/20ft 3in
  Height – 3.11m/10ft 3in
  Width – 3.24m/10ft 8in
**Armament:** Main – 155mm/6.1in M45 howitzer
  Secondary – 12.7mm/0.5in machine-gun
**Armour:** Maximum – 12.7mm/0.5in
**Powerplant:** Continental AOS-895-3 6-cylinder 373kW/500hp petrol engine
**Performance:** Speed – 56kph/35mph
  Range – 122km/76 miles

LEFT: **The crew compartment of the M52 is a covered armoured turret and gives the gun crew full protection from the weather and small-arms fire. The driver of the vehicle sits at the front of the turret. In this picture, he has his seat in the raised position, with the vehicle commander at the rear on the opposite side of the turret.** ABOVE: **The engine is positioned in the front of the vehicle with the exhaust systems on the front track guards. The front of the glacis is covered in air intake grills.**

# M52 105mm Self-Propelled Gun

In February 1948, development was started on a replacement 105mm SPG for the M7 which was showing its age. Two prototypes, known as the T98E1, were built at the Detroit Tank Arsenal in 1950. They were to be constructed using as many parts from the M41 light tank as possible and the engine, transmission, tracks and suspension were all used. The T98E1 was standardized in 1953 as the M52 and entered service in 1954 with a total production run of 684 vehicles. In 1956 a new vehicle with an improved engine and fuel injection system was standardized as the M52A1.

The hull of the M52 was an all-welded steel construction, with the engine and

transmission mounted at the front of the vehicle. The transmission was a General Motors Model CD-500-3 cross-drive unit which gave the vehicle two forward gears and one reverse. The suspension was a torsion-bar system and the rear idler was lowered to form a sixth road wheel. The large turret was mounted on the top of the hull towards the rear of the vehicle. All the crew were seated in the turret with the driver on the front left-hand side with a cupola above and a door in the side of the turret for access to the driving position. The gun layer was on the right-hand side of the turret at the front with the commander behind. The commander's cupola could be fitted with

a 12.7mm/0.3in machine-gun for close defence. On the rear, left-hand side of the turret a revolving drum was fitted which held 21 rounds of ready-to-use ammunition and a total of 102 rounds were carried in the vehicle. The turret had a 60-degree traverse to the left and right of the vehicle's centreline. No recoil spade was fitted to the rear of the vehicle, as it was not required.

The vehicle had no NBC system installed but was fitted with an over-pressurization system and infrared night-driving lights. It was the first NATO SPG to give the crew full protection on the modern nuclear battlefield.

RIGHT: **The compact size of the chassis can be seen, but the large turret takes up most of the space on the top of the vehicle. Driving the vehicle was not easy, but the crews did get used to it. Ammunition is stowed both in the turret and in the body of the vehicle.**

## M52 105mm SPG

**Country:** USA
**Entered service:** 1954
**Crew:** 5
**Weight:** 24,079kg/23.7 tons
**Dimensions:** Length – 5.8m/19ft
　　　　Height – 3.06m/10ft 1in
　　　　Width – 3.15m/10ft 4in
**Armament:** Main – 105mm/4.13in M49 howitzer
　　　　Secondary – 12.7mm/0.5in machine-gun
**Armour:** Maximum – 12.7mm/0.5in
**Powerplant:** Continental 6-cylinder 373kW/500hp petrol engine
**Performance:** Speed – 56kph/35mph
　　　　Range – 160km/100 miles

# M107 175mm Self-Propelled Gun

All SPGs in service in the early 1950s were too large and heavy to be transported by air, but in 1956 the Pacific Car and Foundry Company was awarded a contract to build six prototype air-transportable SPG vehicles, two armed with the new 175mm/6.89in gun, three with the 203mm/8in howitzer and one with the 155mm/6.1in gun. Trials began in late 1958 but the engine was changed in 1959 when the American armed forces made a policy decision that all future vehicles would be fitted with diesel engines rather than petrol. Trials were completed in early 1961. The T235E1 (175mm) was standardized as the M107 and the T236E1 (203mm) as the M110, while the other vehicle was dropped. Production started in 1962 and was completed in 1980 by which time 524 vehicles had been built. After a short period of time in service, a large number of faults were discovered and these were rectified.

The M107 hull is an all-welded construction made from cast armour and high-tensile alloy steel. The driver is positioned in the front of the vehicle on the left-hand side with the engine on the right, while the main gun mount is at the rear of the vehicle. The driver is the only member of the crew to sit inside the vehicle and therefore be protected by armour. The torsion-bar suspension has five twin rubber tyre wheels per side with the drive sprocket at the front and the fifth road wheel acting as an idler. There is a shock absorber fitted to each road wheel and this helps transfer the recoil shock directly into the ground. In

ABOVE: **The M107 returned to the idea that artillery was not in the front line, so crew protection was not needed. The large full-width recoil spade can be seen in the raised position on the rear of this vehicle.**

LEFT: **The extremely long gun barrel stands out well in this picture. The driver and two of the crew can be seen in their travelling positions on the gun. The other two members of the gun crew were on the other side of the gun mount.**

addition there is a hydraulically operated recoil spade at the rear of the vehicle.

The M107 has a crew of 13; 4 of them – including the vehicle commander – travel on the vehicle with the driver inside, the other 8 are transported in an M548 ammunition vehicle. The M107 has internal storage space for only two ready-to-use 175mm/6.89in rounds

and the barrel of the 175mm/6.89in gun can be interchanged with the M110 203mm/8in barrel. This operation takes two hours and can be undertaken in the field.

LEFT: **Two M107 guns on exercise. The gun in the rear has just fired a round, while the vehicle in the foreground is on the move with the five-man crew at their travelling stations. The barrel of the gun has been covered in camouflage netting.**

## M107 175mm SPG

**Country:** USA
**Entered service:** 1963
**Crew:** 4 plus 9 gunners
**Weight:** 28,143kg/27.7 tons
**Dimensions:** Length – 11.26m/36ft 11in
   Height – 3.67m/12ft
   Width – 3.15m/10ft 4in
**Armament:** Main – 175mm/6.89in M113 gun
   Secondary – Small arms
**Armour:** Classified
**Powerplant:** Detroit Diesel Motors 8V-71T
   8-cylinder 302kW/405hp diesel engine
**Performance:** Speed – 55kph/34mph
   Range – 725km/450 miles

# M108 105mm Self-Propelled Gun

Take a 22,353kg/22-ton aluminium armoured vehicle and mount a relatively small 105mm/4.13in howitzer on it, and the result would appear to be a massively under-gunned self-propelled howitzer. A clean and simple design, the M108 represented a more sophisticated approach than the M52 but, not surprisingly, was only built in small numbers.

Development started in 1953 when it was decided to develop a 110mm/4.33in-armed SPG which was designated the T195. The first mock-up vehicle was built in 1954. Permission was subsequently given for prototype vehicles to be built and orders were placed for engines and transmissions. However, later that year it was decided to freeze the project, as there were doubts over the 110mm/4.33in gun. The engines and other parts were passed over to the T196/M109 project. It was

ABOVE: The large size of the vehicle can be seen against the small size of the gun barrel. The 12.7mm/0.5in machine-gun can be seen on the roof of the turret. BELOW LEFT: This was the first turreted SPG to have the driver placed in the hull of the vehicle. The box on the rear of the turret is the air filtration system for the NBC system. These vehicles were produced for less than a year. BELOW: The M108 chassis was used for the American trials of the Roland Low-Altitude SAM system. It was converted in 1977 and the first firing trials were carried out in November 1977. The vehicle has a crew of four. From shut-down to fully operational takes under four minutes.

finally decided to drop the 110mm/4.33in gun in favour of the 105mm/4.13in, as there was a plentiful supply of ammunition for this weapon. The first prototype was finally completed in 1958 but the suspension failed in its first firing trials. When the

American military ordered in 1959 that all vehicles were to have diesel engines fitted as standard from now on, the T195 had its petrol engine replaced by a diesel unit and was given the new designation T195E1. Trials started again, with suspension failures being repeated, but this time they were corrected, and in 1961 the T195E1 was finally standardized as the M108. Production started in October 1962 after a number of changes to the design including the addition of an idler wheel at the rear of the vehicle, the removal of the muzzle brake and changes to the turret shape. The very short production run finished in September 1963 with only a few vehicles completed, production being halted because the US military decided to concentrate on the T196/M109 155mm/6.1in SPG, a unit that is still in service today.

The hull and turret of the M108 is an all-welded aluminium construction. The transmission is located in the front of the vehicle with the driver behind this on the left-hand side and the engine on the right. The torsion-bar suspension system of the M108 is the same as that of the M113 with seven dual rubber-shod road wheels per side. The drive sprocket is at the front of the vehicle and an idler is at the rear. The top of the tracks can be covered with a rubber skirt but the crews rarely fit this.

At the rear of the vehicle is the manually operated turret which can rotate through 360 degrees and houses the rest of

the crew and the gun. The gun-layer is on the left-hand side of this with the commander on the right, while the two ammunition handlers are positioned in the rear. In the roof of the turret above the commander is a cupola, and this can be traversed through 360 degrees and can be armed with a 12.7mm/0.5in local defence machine-gun. The gun-layer also has a hatch in the roof of the turret, and two side hatches which open towards the rear of the vehicle are also fitted. In the rear of the turret are two more hatches in the rotating top section, while in the lower fixed rear of the hull a large door is installed which is used for supplying ammunition to the gun. The M108 carries 87 rounds of ammunition. The vehicle is capable of firing three rounds per minute but this is only for a short period of time, the normal fire rate being one round per minute.

The M108 can be fitted with an NBC system but this is not fitted as standard, though infrared night-driving lights are. The vehicle can wade to a depth of 1.8m/5ft 11in but can also be fitted with nine flotation bags, one bag on the front and four down each side, which are inflated from the vehicle. However, these are not carried on the vehicle as standard. Propulsion in the water is supplied by the vehicle's tracks. Although an unmitigated failure in its original role and long out of service with the US Army, the Belgian Army has converted several of its M108 SPGs into command vehicles.

ABOVE LEFT: **Only three other countries bought the M108: Belgium, Brazil and Spain. Belgium turned out to be the largest overseas customer.** ABOVE: **The very short length of the barrel can be clearly seen. The drive sprocket is at the front of the vehicle, which makes for a very compact drive train. The engine and drive train proved to be very reliable and were used in several vehicles.** LEFT: **The first vehicles had the headlight cluster mounted on the glacis plate, but on later production vehicles the headlights were moved to the front of the track guards.**

### M108 105mm SPG

**Country:** USA
**Entered service:** 1962
**Crew:** 5
**Weight:** 22,454kg/22.1 tons
**Dimensions:** Length – 6.11m/20ft 9in
 Height – 3.15m/10ft 4in
 Width – 3.3m/10ft 10in
**Armament:** Main – 105mm/4.13in M103 howitzer
 Secondary – 12.7mm/0.5in M2 machine-gun
**Armour:** Classified
**Powerplant:** Detroit Diesel Motors 8V-71T
 8-cylinder 302kW/405hp diesel engine
**Performance:** Speed – 55kph/34mph
 Range – 350km/220 miles

# M109 155mm Self-Propelled Gun

The first prototype M109, then designated the T196, was finally completed in 1959 but during its first firing trials the suspension failed. When in the same year the American military ordered that all future new vehicles were to have diesel engines fitted as standard, the petrol engine was replaced by a diesel and the vehicle was given the new designation T196E1. Trials started again and again there were suspension failures, as with the M108 which had the same chassis. These problems were corrected and the first vehicles were completed in October 1962 as Limited Production Vehicles. Finally, in 1963 the T196E1 was standardized as the M109. A number of changes were made to the design including the addition of an idler wheel at the rear of the vehicle and changes to the turret shape before the M109 entered service with the American Army in June 1963. It will remain in service until at least 2010, but the vehicle has gone through many changes and upgrades during its service life to keep it up-to-date.

The hull and turret of the M109 is an all-welded aluminium construction. The transmission is in the front of the vehicle with the driver located behind this on the left-hand side. The engine is next to the driver on the right, and the turret, which houses the rest of the crew and gun, is behind. The gun-layer is positioned on the left-hand side of the turret with the commander on the right. A cupola for the commander, which can be traversed through 360 degrees and can be armed with a 12.7mm/0.5in local defence machine-gun, is installed in the roof of the turret. The gun-layer also has a hatch in the roof of the turret, and two side hatches, which open towards the rear

of the vehicle, are also fitted. In the rear of the turret are two more hatches in the rotating top section, and there is a large door in the rear of the hull which is used for supplying ammunition to the gun. Mounted on the rear of the vehicle is a large recoil spade that is manually operated from within the turret. The main armament is the M126 155mm/6.1in gun on the M127 mount. The barrel is fitted with a double-baffle muzzle brake and a fume extractor two-thirds of the way up. The turret can traverse through 360 degrees and is power operated, but can be operated manually. The normal rate of fire is one round per minute but for short periods, three rounds per minute can be fired. The latest version of the vehicle, the M109A6 Paladin, is armed with the M284 L/39 155mm/6.1in howitzer and a new fire-control system.

LEFT: **A Swiss Army M109A2. On the roof of this vehicle is a new armoured hood for the optical fire-control system. This vehicle is known as the Pzhb 74 in the Swiss Army.** ABOVE: **A British M109A2 vehicle taking part in a live-firing exercise. The optical hood is on the front left of the turret. The turret of the M109A2 is fitted with a bustle that can hold an additional 22 rounds of ammunition. The gun has been heavily covered in camouflage netting and spare ammunition is laid out on a sheet behind the gun.**

The first improvements were made to the vehicle in 1972 and it was redesignated the M109A1. These were mainly to the gun that had a much longer and more slender barrel increasing the range to 18,288m/60,000ft. Further developments came in 1978 when the M109A2 went into production, with improvements to the ammunition storage, the rammer, and hull doors. A bustle was also fixed to the rear of the turret to take a further 22 rounds of ammunition. The M109A3 upgrade was M109A1s brought up to M109A2 standard. The vehicle became the M109A4 in 1990 with the fitting of an NBC kit as standard. The M109A5 designation was the upgrading of all the older marks to A4 standard, and the gun barrel was also changed to one that could fire rocket-assisted ammunition.

The latest version of the M109 is the A6 Paladin. Development of this started in 1990 and production began in 1992 with the new vehicle entering service with the American Army in 1993. The Paladin has the same chassis and hull as the basic M109 but everything else has been changed. The turret is bigger, the

rear doors in the upper part of the turret have been removed, as the bustle is now full width, and there is also a new muzzle brake. A new gun-control system has been fitted which is linked to a GPS (Global Positioning System), allowing the automatic gun controls to point the gun at the target with no human intervention.

ABOVE: **A line-up of American M109A6 vehicles. The M109A6 is better known as the "Paladin", and is the first vehicle in the series to be given a name. The large muzzle brake has a double baffle, and behind this on the barrel of the gun is the fume extractor.** LEFT: **This vehicle is fording a stream at some speed. The M109 can ford water obstacles to a depth of 1m/39in. The vehicle commander can be seen standing in his cupola giving directions to the driver, who has very poor vision from his position.**

## M109A6 155mm Paladin SPG

**Country:** USA
**Entered service:** 1993
**Crew:** 6
**Weight:** 28,753kg/28.3 tons
**Dimensions:** Length – 9.12m/29ft 11in
 Height – 3.24m/10ft 7in
 Width – 3.15m/10ft 4in
**Armament:** Main – 155mm/6.1in M284 L/39 howitzer
 Secondary – 12.7mm/0.5in M2 machine-gun
**Armour:** classified
**Powerplant:** Detroit Diesel Motors 8V-71T 8-cylinder 302kW/405hp diesel engine
**Performance:** Speed – 56kph/35mph
 Range – 405km/252 miles

LEFT: **The gun crew of the M110 are very exposed when operating the gun, as can be seen with this vehicle. The recoil spade on this SPG is in the down position.** BELOW: **A line-up of three batteries of M110 vehicles. The gun has no muzzle brake or fume extractor. The vehicle can carry 5 of the 13-man crew; the rest travel in an M548 ammunition vehicle.**

# M110 203mm Self-Propelled Howitzer

In 1956 the Pacific Car and Foundry Company (PCF) was given a contract to build six prototype SPG vehicles for the US Army, two armed with the new 175mm/6.89in gun (T235), three with the 203mm/8in howitzer (T236) and one with the 155mm/6.1in gun (T245). The main design priority for these vehicles was that they all had to be air-portable to fill a requirement not met by the then available American SPGs, which were either too large or too heavy. The three prototype designs all used the same M17 lightweight gun mount and were all to have the ability for their gun barrels to be interchangeable. The T245 development was halted at the prototype stage as it was felt to be unnecessary. The T235 went on to become the M107, while the T236 became the M110. The M108, M109 and M110 all utilized the same transmission and engine.

Testing of the M110 prototype began in late 1958 but in 1959 the American military made a policy decision that all future vehicles would be fitted with diesel engines rather than petrol. The T236 with a diesel engine fitted was renamed the T236E1. Trials were completed in 1961 and the T236E1 was standardized as the M110. In June 1961, PCF was awarded a production contract for the new vehicle and the first production models were finished in 1962, entering service with the US Army in 1963. The original contract was for 750 vehicles, all built by PCF, which were completed by late 1969. Once the vehicle had entered service, it was found that improvements to the engine-cooling, electrical and hydraulic systems, the loader/rammer and the recoil spade were necessary. In March 1976, an improved vehicle incorporating these modifications was standardized as the M110A1. These vehicles included

RIGHT: **The eight circular holes in the right-hand side of the vehicle are the exhaust outlets. This caused a lot of discomfort for the crew of the vehicle when it was stationary. The short, stubby gun barrel can be clearly seen on this SPG.**

both M110s and some M107s, as a number of M107 vehicles were no longer required. A new longer gun barrel, the M201, was fitted to the vehicle so it could fire tactical nuclear shells as the M107 had done and which the M110A1 would eventually replace. In 1980, the last version of the M110 entered service, as the M110A2. This had an improved barrel and was fitted with a muzzle brake. Improvements were also made to the electrical and recoil systems. With this last upgrade the gun crew at long last had some protection from small-arms fire, shell splinters and the weather, as a Kevlar and aluminium shelter was built over the open gun area.

The M110 hull is an all-welded construction made from cast armour and high tensile alloy steel. The driver is located in the front of the vehicle on the left-hand side with the engine on the right, while the main gun mount is at the rear. The driver is the only member of the crew to sit inside the vehicle and therefore be protected by armour. The torsion-bar suspension has five twin rubber-tyred wheels per side with the drive sprocket at the front and the fifth road wheel acting as an idler. There is a shock absorber fitted to each road wheel and this helps transfer the recoil shock directly into the ground. There is also a hydraulically operated recoil spade at the rear. On the right-hand side of the vehicle are a series of holes in the sponson that act as exhaust outlets.

The vehicle commander and three members of the gun crew sit in the open, two either side, exposed to small-arms fire, shell splinters and above all the weather. The other eight crewmen are transported in an M548 ammunition vehicle along with all the personal kit of the gun crew. The main armament is fitted with a hydro-pneumatic recoil system and an automatic loader and rammer is located at the rear of the vehicle on the left-hand side. The M110 only has storage for two ready-to-use rounds, the remaining being carried in the ammunition vehicle. The normal rate of fire is one round every two minutes, but for short periods, two rounds per minute can be fired. The M110A2 is the only variation still in service and this is with a small number of countries.

TOP: **An American M110 with the recoil spade in the raised position. One improvement the Americans made to this vehicle was the construction of a canvas tent around the exposed gun position on the rear of the vehicle.** ABOVE: **The M110 has five road wheels on each side and the drive sprocket is at the front. No return roller is fitted to the chassis.** BELOW LEFT: **These vehicles are the improved M110A1. They have much longer barrels but still no muzzle brake or fume extractor fitted; the M110A2 would have a large double-baffle muzzle brake. These M110A1 SPGs are at maximum elevation and the hoop frame of the canvas screen can be seen.**

| M110A2 203mm SPG | 🇺🇸 |
|---|---|
| **Country:** USA | |
| **Entered service:** 1980 | |
| **Crew:** 5 plus 8 gunners | |
| **Weight:** 28,346kg/27.9 tons | |
| **Dimensions:** Length – 7.5m/24ft 7in<br>　　Height – 3.15m/10ft 4in<br>　　Width – 3.15m/10ft 4in | |
| **Armament:** Main – 203mm/8in M12A2 howitzer<br>　　Secondary – Small arms | |
| **Armour:** Classified | |
| **Powerplant:** Detroit Diesel Motors 8V-71T<br>　　8-cylinder 373kW/500hp diesel engine | |
| **Performance:** Speed – 55kph/34mph<br>　　Range – 523km/325 miles | |

LEFT: **An American M113 fitted with a TOW AT missile launcher. The vehicle commander's hatch is open, but the position is empty. This APC has been fitted with rubber track guards.**
ABOVE: **A basic American M113 APC. The driver is in his position in the front of the vehicle on the left-hand side. The vehicle commander's position has been fitted with a 12.7mm/0.5in machine-gun.**

# M113 Armoured Personnel Carrier

In January 1956 the Food Manufacturing Corporation (FMC) were awarded a contract to start development on the T113 and the T117 APCs. These new vehicles had to be fully air-portable, amphibious, lightweight and have a good cross-country performance. They had to be adaptable and be able to take modification kits with a long projected service life. Testing started and the steel-bodied T117 was quickly dropped in favour of the aluminium-constructed T113. The T113E1 was developed with a petrol engine and four prototypes were built, but the diesel-engined T113E2 was also developed following the US Army's 1959 requirement for diesel engines in all its new vehicles. Despite this, the T113E1 was standardized in 1960 as the M113 and FMC began production with an order for 900 vehicles, all with petrol engines. In 1963 the diesel-engined T113E2 was standardized as the M113A1 and entered production in 1964, replacing the basic M113.

The next version of the M113, the M113A2, entered production in 1978. This involved a number of improvements to the engine-cooling system, radiator, and suspension. All M113s and M113A1s were also to be brought up to the same standard, involving some 20,000 vehicles, and a further 2,660 new M113A2s were to be built. The whole programme had to be finished by 1989. In 1980 development started on a further improvement programme including a new engine, giving better performance, and improved cooling and suspension systems. Production of the new M113A3 began in 1987 and is still continuing today. It includes improvements such as external fuel tanks and the provision for the installation of external

ABOVE: **This Israeli M113 has been fitted with additional add-on armour. The crew of the vehicle are at action stations. The trim vane has been removed to allow the armour to be fitted.**

optional appliqué armour. Experience gained in the Gulf War of 1991 has influenced a number of these developments.

The hull of the M113 is an all-welded aluminium construction. The transmission, providing six forward and two reverse gears, is in the front of the vehicle. The driver sits behind this on the left-hand side, with the engine immediately on the right. The air inlet and outlet louvers for the engine are located on the roof of the hull. The commander's position is in the centre of the vehicle, and is provided with a cupola that can be traversed through 360 degrees and is fitted with a single

LEFT: **This is an M113 armed with a TOW AT missile. The TOW is mounted on a pedestal mount, which when not in use is retracted inside the hull and covered by the large hatches on the roof of the vehicle.** BELOW: **An Israeli M113 in a combat area in the Middle East. The vehicle is armed with a TOW missile and two 12.5mm/50cal machine-guns. The front machine-gun is mounted over the commander's hatch. The M113 is covered in extra storage racks that have been added by the crew.**

M2 12.7mm/0.5in machine-gun. In the rear of the vehicle is the troop compartment with accommodation for 11 men. These sit five down each side facing each other, with one single seat behind the vehicle commander. A large single hatch which opens to the rear of the vehicle covers the troop compartment. In the rear is the main entry and exit hatch that is a hydraulic ramp, with an integral door fitted to the left-hand side for use in the event of the ramp mechanism failing. The vehicle is fully amphibious and is ready to enter the water once the trim vane at the front of the vehicle has been raised. Propulsion in the water is provided by using its tracks.

In 2005 the M113A3 fleet had some 16 different models in service with the US Army and many others around the world. The vehicle has been modified into 40 specific variations with a further 40 unofficial variations and is the most widely produced, in-service vehicle in the Western World. The basic armament is a single 12.7mm/0.5in machine-gun, but after this, whatever is required seems to have been fitted to the vehicle. Cannon such as 20mm/0.79in and 30mm/1.18in and even up to a 90mm/3.54in-armed turret have been fitted, as well as various missile systems. The vehicle does possess one rather alarming fault which has not been eliminated despite numerous

improvements. If it loses a track or breaks a track shoe then extreme care must be taken when slowing the vehicle. Use of the foot brake or any other means of braking can cause the vehicle to pull to the side of the unbroken track and roll over.

The M113 family has been in production for a long time and some 80,000 of all types have been built. This vehicle is still a good basic reliable battlefield taxi and is well liked by its crews. In 2005, it was in service with 52 different countries and is expected to remain so for a further 10 to 15 years.

LEFT: **This basic M113 is travelling across rough ground at speed. A number of countries have improved the armament of their basic M113 vehicles by adding various turrets. The largest of these is the 90mm/3.54in Cockerill Mk III turret.**

| M113A3 APC |  |
| --- | --- |

**Country:** USA
**Entered service:** 1987
**Crew:** 2 plus 11 infantry
**Weight:** 12,339kg/12.1 tons
**Dimensions:** Length – 4.86m/15ft 11in
 Height – 2.52m/8ft 3in
 Width – 2.69m/8ft 10in
**Armament:** Main – 12.7mm/0.5in M2 HB
 machine-gun
 Secondary – Small arms
**Armour:** Maximum – 38mm/1.5in
**Powerplant:** Detroit Diesel model 6V53T
 6-cylinder 205kW/275hp
**Performance:** Speed – Road 65kph/41mph;
 Water 5.8kph/3.6mph
 Range – 497km/309 miles

LEFT: **This M577 has had a wire-mesh storage basket fitted to the front of the vehicle next to the driver. Even with the increased height of the vehicle, the M577 retains its amphibious capability, hence this vehicle has its trim vane fitted to the front.** ABOVE: **An American M577 command vehicle, with an M60 MBT behind it. The driver has his hatch open and the vehicle commander is standing in his hatch in the roof of the vehicle.**

# M577 Command Vehicle

Once the basic M113 had entered production, FMC started development of the command post variant. Production commenced in 1962 and the first M577, the first true command post vehicle developed for the US Army, entered service in 1963. The M577 has gone through the same upgrades as the M113 APC with numerous improvements to the cooling and suspension systems, the driving controls and the engine. The M577A3 has also had the auxiliary petrol APU replaced with a 5kW/6.7hp diesel-powered unit. The first upgrade in 1964 produced the M577A1. In 2005, the vehicle in service was the M577A3 and this is expected to remain operational for 10 to 15 years. The US Army originally bought 944 M577 vehicles and they have purchased a further 2,693 M577A1 since 1964.

The hull of the M557 is an all-welded aluminium construction. The transmission is located in the front and provides the vehicle with six forward and two reverse gears. The driver sits behind the transmission at the front of the vehicle on the left-hand side, with the engine located on the right. Air inlet and outlet louvers for the engine are located on the roof of the hull. Behind the driver is the crew area, with a roof that is raised more than 91cm/3ft higher than the original hull top. This allows the command crew to work in the rear of the vehicle and provides the extra space required for the additional communication equipment. On the front of the raised crew area is the APU, and there is a cupola that can be fitted with an M2 12.7mm/0.5in machine-gun in the roof of the crew area for use by the vehicle commander.

In addition to its use as a command post, the M577A3 is used for several other tasks such as a fire-direction centre, field treatment centre and a communications vehicle. In 2005, the XM577A4 was under development, which is a stretched version of the M113. This lengthens the vehicle by 66cm/2ft 2in, and increases the payload to over 2,268kg/5,000lb. The vehicle's increased length means that an extra pair of road wheels had to be fitted to the vehicle.

LEFT: **The increased height and bulk of the M577 can be clearly seen, compared to the original M113 APC. The top of this vehicle is covered in personal equipment. A number of these vehicles have been converted into mobile medical units.**

## M577A3 Command Vehicle

**Country:** USA
**Entered service:** 1987
**Crew:** 4
**Weight:** 14,424kg/14.2 tons
**Dimensions:** Length – 4.86m/15ft 11in
　Height – 3.89m/12ft 9in
　Width – 2.69m/8ft 10in
**Armament:** Main – 7.62mm/0.3in M60 machine-gun
　Secondary – Small arms
**Armour:** Maximum – 38mm/1.5in
**Powerplant:** Detroit Diesel model 6V53T 6-cylinder 205kW/275hp diesel engine
**Performance:** Speed – Road 65kph/41mph;
　Water 5.8kph/3.6mph
　Range – 497km/309 miles

LEFT: **An M901 with the TOW launcher in the reload position. A member of the crew is feeding a missile into the rear of the launcher. Two missiles are carried in the launcher while ten others are carried in the body of the vehicle.** BELOW: **An M901 with its TOW launcher in the raised position. The turret can traverse through 360 degrees, and can elevate to 34 degrees. When on the move, the turret can be retracted so that it sits on the roof of the vehicle.**

# M901 Improved TOW Vehicle

By 1979, the US Army had some 1,400 TOW-armed vehicles in service. These first TOW (Tube-launched, Optically-tracked, Wire-guided) vehicles were basic M113 APCs fitted with a pedestal-mounted weapon system that retracted into the troop compartment. However, development work was started in 1976 on a new and better Improved TOW Vehicle (ITV) system that could be fitted to the M113A2 vehicle; this would become the M901A1. The M901 would be developed in the same way as the M113 and went through the same upgrades of suspension, cooling, driving controls and engine. In 2005, the vehicle in service was the M901A3 and this has all the improvements of the M113A3 plus some additional improvements such as

M17 laser protection and enhanced armour protection. Production of the M901 started in 1979. The US Army had a requirement for 2,526 of these vehicles, and 1,100 of these vehicles were deployed in Europe by 1981.

The hull of the M901 is an all-welded aluminium construction. The transmission, giving six forward and two reverse gears, is located in the front of the vehicle. The driver sits behind the transmission at the front of the vehicle on the left-hand side, with the engine on the right. Behind the driver and engine position is an M27 cupola. This is fitted with an image-transfer system, armoured launcher, missile guidance equipment and an auxiliary back-up battery pack. Two

TOW missile tubes are fitted to the armoured launcher, the acquisition sight is mounted on the top and between the TOW tubes is the TOW sight. A further 10 TOW missiles are carried inside the vehicle. Behind the M27 cupola is a large hatch that provides access to the TOW launcher so that spent missile tubes can be removed and jettisoned over the side of the vehicle allowing reloading to take place. Once the vehicle comes to a halt the TOW launcher is raised to the firing height and the first target engaged. This takes 20 seconds and reloading can be completed in 40 seconds. When in the travelling mode the launcher is retracted and sits on the hull roof, making the vehicle more difficult to identify.

RIGHT: **A US Marine Corps vehicle heading into the water. The launcher turret is built by Emerson. This is made up of the M27 cupola, image-transfer equipment, armoured launcher, missile guidance set and a battery back-up pack.**

### M901A3 ITV

**Country:** USA
**Entered service:** 1989
**Crew:** 3
**Weight:** 12,339kg/12.1 tons
**Dimensions:** Length – 4.86m/15ft 11in
    Height – 3.36m/11ft
    Width – 2.69m/8ft 10in
**Armament:** Main – TOW launcher
    Secondary – 7.62mm/0.3in M60 machine-gun
**Armour:** Maximum – 38mm/1.5in
**Powerplant:** Detroit Diesel model 6V53T
    6-cylinder 205kW/275hp diesel engine
**Performance:** Speed – Road 65kph/41mph;
    Water 5.8kph/3.6mph
    Range – 497km/309 miles

# Marder 1 Infantry Combat Vehicle

In the late 1950s, development started on a chassis that could be used for a family of military vehicles for the Federal German Army. The first vehicles in the series required by the German Army were the tank destroyers – the Jagdpanzer Kanone and Jagdpanzer Rakete. The Kanone entered production in 1965 while the Rakete entered production in 1967, and both were still in service in 2005. The next vehicle to be developed was the Infantry Combat Vehicle (ICV). The contracts were issued in 1960 to three companies to be involved in prototype production; Rheinstahl-Hanomag, Henschel and MOWAG. Between 1961 and 1963, a second series of prototype vehicles were built and the final series of prototype vehicles were produced in 1967–68. In April 1969, the three companies were invited to tender for the production of the ICV. In May 1969, the new vehicle was given the name Marder, and Rheinstahl-Hanomag won the contract. The first production vehicles were completed in December 1970, but

did not officially enter service with the Federal German Army until May 1971. In total, 3,100 Marder 1 ICVs were produced.

The hull of the Marder is an all-welded aluminium construction, and provides protection from small-arms fire and shell splinters. The front of the Marder is proof against direct fire from 20mm/0.79in ammunition. The driver sits at the front of the vehicle on the left-hand side and has a single-piece hatch in front of which are three vision blocks. Next to the driver on the right-hand side is the engine; the radiators for this are mounted on the rear of the vehicle on either side of the ramp. Behind the driver is the squad commander who has a hatch in the roof of the vehicle.

The two-man turret is mounted on the centreline just behind the squad commander and engine. The vehicle commander sits in the turret on the right-hand side with the gunner on the left. Both have their own hatches in the turret and the

LEFT: **This Marder is taking part in a NATO exercise in Germany. The crew of the Marder are servicing their vehicle's armament, while the vehicle itself is covered in camouflage netting.** ABOVE: **Six smoke dischargers are fitted to the main support arm of the 20mm/0.79in cannon. In the side of the infantry compartment are two MOWAG ball mountings for the infantry to fire their weapons from inside the vehicle.**

commander has all-round vision from eight different vision blocks. The 20mm/0.79in Rheinmetall MK20 Rh202 cannon is mounted externally on the vehicle and can traverse through 360 degrees. The cannon is fed from two different ammunition belts which can be loaded with different types of ammunition and has a rate of fire of 800–1,000 rounds per minute. The vehicle carries 1,250 rounds of ammunition for this main gun. Mounted coaxially on the left hand side of the turret is a 7.62mm/0.3in machine-gun.

In the rear of the vehicle is the troop compartment with accommodation for six men sitting in the middle of the compartment, three on each side, facing outwards. There are also two firing ports on each side and four hatches in the roof. The main exit and entrance to the troop compartment is via a power-operated ramp that folds down from the top of the vehicle. A remote-controlled 7.62mm/0.3in machine-gun with a traverse of 180 degrees was originally fitted above the troop compartment at the rear of the vehicle, but this has now been removed on many vehicles. All Marder vehicles in German Army service have now been fitted with the MILAN anti-tank guided missile and a full NBC system.

In 1982 the Marder went through an upgrade programme which improved the main armament, night-vision lights, thermal pointer, and NBC system and gave better personal equipment stowage in the troop compartment. This vehicle became the Marder A1. The Marder A1A was also produced having all the same improvements the A1 except the improved night-vision equipment. The Germans brought 670 Marder vehicles up to A1 standard and 1,400 vehicles to the A1A standard. In 2005, the vehicle in service was the Marder 1A3, and all Marders have now been brought up to this standard, with improved armour and new improved roof hatches. A new vehicle, the Marder 2, was due to enter production in 1995, but with the demolition of the Berlin Wall and the unification of Germany, a large number of military projects have been cancelled due to a dramatic cutback in military budgets, among them the Marder 2. The Marder ICV is only in service with the German Army but the chassis has been used to mount the Roland Surface-to-Air Missile system which came into service in 2005 with several countries in the NATO Alliance.

LEFT: **The infantry section of this Marder are boarding their vehicle. The rear ramp is not fully lowered. A MILAN AT missile launcher has been fitted to the side of the main turret, which can traverse through 360 degrees and has a maximum elevation of 65 degrees.**

## Marder 1 ICV

**Country:** West Germany
**Entered service:** 1971
**Crew:** 3 plus 6 infantry
**Weight:** 29,210kg/28.75 tons
**Dimensions:** Length – 6.79m/22ft 3in
   Height – 2.98m/9ft 9in
   Width – 3.24m/10ft 7in
**Armament:** Main – 20mm/0.79in MK20 Rh202 cannon, and coaxial 7.62mm/0.3in machine-gun
   Secondary – Small arms
**Armour:** Classified
**Powerplant:** MTU MB 833 Ea-500 6-cylinder 447kW/600hp diesel engine
**Performance:** Speed – 75kph/46mph
   Range – 520km/325 miles

LEFT: **This Marksman turret is fitted on a Chieftain chassis. The large adapter ring on which the turret sits has been designed to fit a number of tanks from other countries.**

BELOW: **The large ventilator grill is visible in the rear of the turret. The height and bulk of the turret can also be clearly seen.**

# Marksman Self-Propelled Anti-Aircraft Gun

The Marksman twin 35mm/1.38in turret was developed by Marconi Command and Control Systems as a private venture and was very similar in concept to the German 35mm/1.38in Gepard. The Marksman system had to be able to function at any time of the day or night and in all weather conditions. Development started in 1983 and the first prototype was finished in time to go on display at the British Army Equipment Exhibition in 1984, where it was shown mounted on a Vickers Mk 3 MBT (Main Battle Tank) chassis. The second prototype was completed in 1986 and was an all-welded steel construction; the turret was built by Vickers and the guns by Oerlikon.

The turret has been designed to be fitted to some 11 different MBT chassis, both NATO and ex-Warsaw Pact, and is easily fitted to this wide range of vehicles by using an adaptor ring where necessary. The only other part required is an electrical and communication interface so the turret crew can talk to the driver of the vehicle. The turret provides the crew with protection from bullets and shell splinters; the commander sits on the left-hand side with the gunner on the right. Both have all-round vision periscopes as well as a roof-mounted gyro-stabilized sight for optically acquired air or ground targets, while the gunner also has a laser range finder. In the rear of the turret is a diesel APU that is the main power supply to the turret.

The main armament is the Oerlikon 35mm/1.38in KDA cannon and one is mounted on each side of the turret. Each gun is supplied with 250 rounds, 20 of them anti-tank. The ammunition is containerized and so reloading of the turret can be completed in 10 minutes. The guns are fully gyro-stabilized, allowing the Marksman to engage targets when the vehicle is on the move. To the rear of the turret roof is an ECM-resistant tracking and surveillance radar which has a range of 12km/7.5 miles. The only country to buy the Marksman is Finland which uses it on the T-55 MBT chassis.

LEFT: **The search radar is fitted to the rear of the turret, and stands 1m/39in above the top of this. Behind each gun barrel on both sides of the turret are a cluster of smoke dischargers.**

## Marksman 35mm SPAAG on Chieftain Chassis

**Country:** UK
**Entered service:** 1987
**Crew:** 3
**Weight:** 54,864kg/54 tons
**Dimensions:** Length – 8.13m/26ft 8in
    Height – 3.07m/10ft 1in
    Width – 3.5m/11ft 6in
**Armament:** Main – 2 x 35mm/1.38in KDA cannon
    Secondary – 7.62mm/0.3in machine-gun
**Armour:** Classified
**Powerplant:** Leyland 12-cylinder 559kW/750hp multi-fuel engine
**Performance:** Speed – 48kph/30mph
    Range – 500km/310 miles

LEFT: An MT-LB fitted with a SNAR 10 counter-battery radar. The SNAR 10 has the NATO codename of "Big Fred". The radar is fitted in a turret sited at the rear of the vehicle. The radar dish is in the raised position but when travelling the dish is folded down on top of the radar turret. The driver's and the vehicle commander/gunner's front visors are in the open position. ABOVE: A crew member is entering the front compartment of the vehicle. This compartment holds two: the driver and vehicle commander, while in the rear of the vehicle there is space for 11 men.

# MT-LB Infantry Carrier

In the late 1960s the Soviet Army required a replacement for the ageing AT-P armoured tracked artillery tractor, so a new vehicle based on the MT-L unarmoured tracked amphibious carrier was developed and called the MT-LB. Production started at the Kharkov Tractor Plant in the late 1969 and it was seen in public for the first time in 1970. The new vehicle can fill many roles including APC, prime mover for 100mm/3.94in AT guns and 122mm/4.8in howitzers, command and radio communication vehicles, and cargo carrier. It is also very good at crossing difficult terrain such as snow or swamp, and is still in service with 14 different countries.

The MT-LB is an all-welded steel construction, and gives the crew protection from small-arms fire and shell splinters. The crew compartment is in the front and occupies the full width of the vehicle with the driver on the left-hand side and the commander on the right. A manually operated turret, armed with a 7.62mm/0.3in PKT machine-gun is mounted in the roof above the commander's position. Next to the turret in the roof of the crew compartment is the commander's hatch and there is also a hatch above the driver's position. Both the driver and the commander have a windscreen to their front, and these are covered by an armoured flap when in action. The engine is mounted behind the driver, but does not run the full width of the vehicle. The air intake and outlet louvers for this are on the roof. Between the crew compartment and the troop compartment is an aisle which allows access to both compartments. The troops sit down each side of the vehicle facing inwards. There are two hatches in the roof and the main entrance and exit is via two doors in the rear of the vehicle which open outwards.

The MT-LB is fully amphibious and is propelled in the water by its tracks. A trim vane, mounted on the front of the vehicle, is raised before entering the water. This operation only takes a few minutes. The vehicle is fitted with a full NBC system and night-driving equipment.

LEFT: This MT-LB is seen towing a T-12A 100mm/3.94in AT gun during a November Parade. The vehicle could carry the six-man gun crew and ammunition. The twin large hatches in the rear of the roof of the vehicle are visible.

## MT-LB Infantry Carrier

**Country:** USSR
**Entered service:** 1970
**Crew:** 2 plus 11 infantry
**Weight:** 11,887kg/11.7 tons
**Dimensions:** Length – 6.45m/21ft 2in
  Height – 1.86m/6ft 1in
  Width – 2.86m/9ft 5in
**Armament:** Main – 7.62mm/0.3in PKT machine-gun
  Secondary – Small arms
**Armour:** Maximum – 10mm/0.394in
**Powerplant:** YaMZ 238V 8-cylinder 179kW/240hp diesel engine
**Performance:** Speed – 62kph/38mph
  Range – 500km/320 miles

LEFT: **An MLRS firing a salvo of missiles. The missiles are fired one at a time so the vehicle does not become unstable.** ABOVE: **A loaded MLRS at maximum elevation. The armoured louvers in front of the windscreen are in the closed position. The MLRS uses the same chassis as the M2 Bradley, and the Cummins diesel engine is mounted in a small compartment behind the crew cab.**

# Multiple Launch Rocket System

In 1972, the Americans started development on a new rocket system that would use a low-cost rocket and had to be as easy to use as a conventional artillery round. The two main companies involved in the project were Boeing and Vought; each company had to develop a Self-Propelled Launcher Loader (SPLL) and 150 rockets. In 1978 France, West Germany, Italy and the United Kingdom asked to join the project and some changes were made to the rockets. A larger rocket motor was to be fitted and the diameter of the rocket increased to 227mm/ 8.9in. In May 1980, Vought won the competition and were awarded the contract to manufacture the SPLL and rockets. The US Army ordered 491 SPLL and 480 reload vehicles together with 400 rockets, all to be delivered by 1990. These new vehicles would play a major part in the 1991 Gulf War (nicknamed "Steel Rain" by the Iraqi Army), and are expected to remain in service until 2020.

The vehicle uses many of the M2/M3 Bradley automotive components and running gear and is an all-welded aluminium construction. In the front of the vehicle is the three-man armoured cab, which houses the driver on the left, vehicle commander on the right and the gunner in the middle. Entry and exit to the cab is via two side doors, one on each side, and each man has a windscreen which is protected by armoured louvers. Only the vehicle commander has a roof hatch. Behind the armoured cab is the engine housing which is in an armoured box, on the top of which is the main air intake for the engine. Behind this is the main rocket pod, which is mounted on a turntable that allows a traverse of 180 degrees. The rocket pod houses 12 solid fuel rockets which are ripple-fired and can be reloaded in less than 10 minutes.

Various warheads can be fitted to the rockets: high-explosive sub-munitions, anti-tank mines and chemical warheads. The basic M77 rocket has a shelf life of 10 years and contains 644 pre-programmed shaped bomblets.

LEFT: **An MLRS in travelling mode. These vehicles are replacing long-range towed artillery in most modern NATO armies. They are expected to remain in service for the next 20 years.**

| MLRS | 🇺🇸 |
| --- | --- |
| **Country:** USA | |
| **Entered service:** 1982 | |
| **Crew:** 3 | |
| **Weight:** 25,191kg/24.8 tons | |
| **Dimensions:** Length – 6.8m/22ft 4in | |
| Height – 2.6m/8ft 6in | |
| Width – 2.92m/9ft 7in | |
| **Armament:** Main – 12 x 227mm/8.9in M77 rockets | |
| Secondary – Small arms | |
| **Armour:** Classified | |
| **Powerplant:** Cummins VTA-903T turbocharged 8-cylinder 373kW/500hp diesel engine | |
| **Performance:** Speed – 64kph/40mph Range – 483km/302 miles | |

# OT-64 Armoured Personnel Carrier

The OT-64 (Obrneny Transporter) 8x8 was jointly developed by Czechoslovakia and Poland, the project starting in 1959. It uses many of the automotive parts of the Tatra 813 heavy truck series and entered service in 1964. The Czechoslovak company Tatra produced the chassis and automotive parts while the Polish firm FSC of Lubin produced the armoured body. The Polish designation for the vehicle was Sredni Kolowy Opancerzny Transporter; OT-64 being the Czech designation. It is still in service with 13 countries.

The hull of the OT-64 is an all-welded steel construction. The crew compartment is in the front of the vehicle, with the driver on the left-hand side and the vehicle commander on the right. Each has a large single door in the side of the vehicle for access to the crew cab and also a hatch in the roof of the compartment. The driver has three vision blocks which provide views to the front and sides. The engine compartment is behind the crew cab and is mounted over the second axle with the air inlet and outlets on the roof and the exhaust pipes on either side of the vehicle. Behind the engine is an octagonal plinth on top of which sits the turret. The turret is operated by one man and has no hatch

in the top of it. To the rear of this is the troop compartment which runs to the rear of the vehicle and has room for eight men inside. At the rear are the main entry and exit doors, both of which are fitted with firing ports. There are four roof hatches above the troop compartment, all of which are also fitted with firing ports, which can be locked in the vertical position and used as shields when using the firing ports. There are also a further two ports in each side of the troop compartment.

The OT-64 is fitted with a basic NBC over-pressure system. Steering is on the front four wheels and the vehicle is fully amphibious, being propelled in the water by two propellers at the rear.

ABOVE: **Three OT-64 APC vehicles taking part in a November Parade. The vehicle commanders are standing in their turrets. Half of the possible eight-man infantry sections are standing in the rear of the vehicles, and the doors of the rear roof hatches have been removed.** LEFT: **An OT-64 being guided around a tight corner. The front four wheels of the vehicle are used for steering, but the turning circle is very large. The exhaust system is fitted to each side of the hull of the vehicle. This APC does not have a turret fitted.**

ABOVE: **The trim vane on this vehicle is folded back against the glacis. The driver's side door is in the open position, folded back against the hull of the vehicle. Above the driver's position is the driver's cupola.**

## OT-64 Armoured Personnel Carrier

**Country:** Czechoslovakia
**Entered service:** 1964
**Crew:** 2 plus 8 infantry
**Weight:** 14,326kg/14.1 tons
**Dimensions:** Length – 7.44m/24ft 5in
    Height – 2m/6ft 6in
    Width – 2.5m/8ft 3in
**Armament:** Main – 14.5mm/0.57in KPVT
    machine-gun, and coaxial 7.62mm/0.3in
    PKT machine-gun
    Secondary – Small arms
**Armour:** Maximum – 14mm/0.55in
**Powerplant:** Tatra 928-14 8-cylinder 134kW/180hp
    diesel engine
**Performance:** Speed – 60kph/37mph
    Range – 500km/310 miles

# OT-810 Armoured Personnel Carrier

During World War II, the Germans manufactured the Sd Kfz 251 half-track at the Skoda plant in Pilsen, Czechoslovakia. After the war had finished, the Czechoslovakian Army were desperate for vehicles and as the Skoda factory was tooled up for Sd Kfz production, they started to make the vehicle again. The first vehicles, unchanged from the basic German design, were delivered in 1948. The first major redesign occurred in the early 1950s when an armoured roof was placed over the troop compartment and the German engine was replaced with a Czech Tatra engine. When the OT-810 was replaced in 1964 on the introduction of the OT-64, a large number of the earlier carriers were converted to anti-tank vehicles. The rear of the vehicle was modified and the gun placed on to it. These variants would remain in service until the late 1980s.

The hull of the vehicle was an all-welded steel construction, with the engine in the front. Behind this was the joint crew and troop compartment. The driver sat in the front of the compartment on the left-hand side, with the vehicle commander, who also acted as the radio operator and gunner, on the right. The driver and commander had small vision

ports to their front and side, and the commander also had a hatch in the roof of the vehicle. The troop compartment held 10 men, five on each side facing each other. In the rear of the vehicle were two large doors that were the sole means of access for the troops and the crew. The OT-810 had neither night-driving equipment nor an NBC system.

The only variant of the OT-810 ever produced was the anti-tank conversion, which had a crew of just four men. This was armed with the M59A recoilless gun,

ABOVE: **The OT-810 was a copy of the World War II German Sd Kfz 251 half-track. The crew compartment has three pistol ports down each side of the hull. The frame above the vehicle commander's position was for a 12.7mm/0.5in heavy machine-gun.**

which was carried in the troop compartment and could be fired from inside the vehicle. Alternatively, it could be dismounted and fired from the ground. Forty rounds of ammunition for this weapon were carried in the vehicle. The twin doors at the rear were removed and replaced with a single hatch.

ABOVE: **The vehicle commander is standing up in his position with the roof hatch folded back. A number of these vehicles are being converted back into Sd Kfz 251s by collectors.**

## OT-810 APC

**Country:** Czechoslovakia
**Entered service:** 1948
**Crew:** 2 plus 10 infantry
**Weight:** 8,534kg/8.4 tons
**Dimensions:** Length – 5.92m/19ft 1in
  Height – 1.75m/5ft 8in
  Width – 2.1m/6ft 9in
**Armament:** Main – 7.62mm/0.3in M59 machine-gun
  Secondary – Small arms
**Armour:** Maximum – 12mm/0.47in
**Powerplant:** Tatra 6-cylinder 89kW/120hp diesel engine
**Performance:** Speed – 52kph/32mph
  Range – 320km/198 miles

LEFT: **This AML 90 car has two unditching channels fitted to the front of the vehicle. On the each side at the rear of the turret are clusters of smoke dischargers. The commander's cupola has a 7.62mm/0.3in machine-gun fitted to the front edge.**

BELOW: **Venezuela is the only country to use this version of the AML. The turret is the S 530 armed with twin 20mm/0.79in cannon. On each side of the turret at the rear is a cluster of smoke dischargers. The large side hatch between the wheels of the vehicle can be clearly seen.**

# Panhard AML 90H Armoured Car

In the late 1950s, the French Army issued a requirement for an armoured car similar to the British Ferret, which they had used in North Africa. Panhard produced the first prototype in 1959 as the Model 245. It passed the trials and was accepted into French Army service as the AML (*AutoMitrailleuse Légère*), the first production vehicle being delivered in 1961. The AML has been built in large numbers, and some 4,800 cars had been produced by 2002. In 2005, it was in service with 39 countries, including France, and production is still available for export customers.

The hull of the AML is an all-welded steel construction. The driver is in the centre front of the vehicle, and has a single hatch that opens to the right.

Behind and above the driver is the turret, which is manufactured by Hispano-Suiza and is armed with the 90mm/3.54in D 921 F1 gun. It also has a 7.62mm/0.3in coaxial machine-gun. The turret houses the vehicle commander on the left-hand side and the gunner on the right; both have hatches in the roof of the turret. There are two large hatches in the sides of the vehicle below the turret, which are the main method of access to the vehicle. The left-hand hatch has the spare wheel mounted on it and opens to the rear while the right-hand door opens towards the front of the vehicle. A 7.62mm/0.3in or 12.7mm/0.5in machine-gun can be mounted on the roof of the vehicle as an anti-aircraft weapon. The engine is in the rear and has two access hatches. Originally the

AML was fitted with a petrol engine but on late production vehicles this has been changed to a diesel unit.

The AML has been produced in many different variants. The body has remained the same but the turret has been changed and fitted with a variety of weapons. These include mountings for 60mm/2.36in mortars and a twin 20mm/0.79in anti-aircraft gun turret. The latest version has an open-topped turret and is known as the AML Scout Car.

LEFT: **The large double-baffle muzzle brake on the end of the barrel is very prominent. The driver has his hatch in the open position. The headlights are mounted under the unditching channels on the front of the vehicle.**

## Panhard AML 90H Armoured Car

**Country:** France
**Entered service:** 1961
**Crew:** 3
**Weight:** 5,486kg/5.4 tons
**Dimensions:** Length – 3.79m/12ft 5in
    Height – 2.07m/6ft 10in
    Width – 1.98m/6ft 6in
**Armament:** Main – 90mm/3.54in D 921 F1 gun,
    and coaxial 7.62mm/0.3in machine-gun
    Secondary – 7.62mm/0.3in machine-gun
**Armour:** Maximum – 12mm/0.47in
**Powerplant:** Panhard Model 4 HD 4-cylinder
    67kW/90hp petrol engine
**Performance:** Speed – 100kph/62mph
    Range – 600km/370 miles

# Panhard ERC-90-F4 Sagaie

Panhard started development of the ERC (*Engin de Reconnaissance Cannon*) in 1975 as a private venture aimed at the export market. The first production vehicles were completed in 1979. The French Army carried out an evaluation between 1978 and 1980 and in December 1980, it was accepted for service. However, further trials were carried out until 1983, the first ERC cars entering French Army service in 1984. An order for 176 ERC-90-F4 Sagaie was placed with the final delivery being made in 1989.

The hull of the ERC is an all-welded steel construction which gives the crew protection from small arms and shell splinters. The hull bottom is made of two plates that are welded together, stiffening the floor and helping protect the vehicle from mines. The driver's position is in the front of the vehicle but is offset to the left-hand side. It can be fitted with night-driving equipment. The two-man turret, armed with a 90mm/3.54in Model 62 F1 gun, is behind and above the driver. The commander is on the left-hand side with the gunner on the right. The commander's cupola has periscopes all round providing a 360-degree field of vision and can also be fitted with a 7.62mm/0.3in or 12.7mm/0.5in machine-gun. The engine is in the rear of the vehicle and is a militarized Peugeot V-6 petrol engine, with six forward and one reverse gear. All six wheels are permanently driven, even the middle pair when raised. The central pair is raised off the ground when the car is driven on hard roads but lowered when traversing rough terrain cross-country.

The ERC range of vehicles use many of the same automotive parts as the VCR series of vehicles. The ERC-90-F4 has a full NBC system and is fully amphibious; normally it is propelled in the water by its wheels but it can be fitted with two water jets mounted at the rear of the vehicle. The vehicle can also be fitted with one of up to ten different turrets.

In 2005, the ERC and its variants were in service with seven different countries, and production can be restarted if necessary.

ABOVE LEFT: **This is the original version armed with the TTB 190 turret, but it is being replaced in service with the French Army by cars fitted with the Lynx turret.** ABOVE: **An ERC-90 fitted with the Lynx turret, which is the same as the one fitted to the AML. Steering is only available via the front wheels of the car. The centre wheels can be raised when travelling on roads.**

LEFT: **Two Lynx-armed vehicles training in the water. The trim vane folds into three and then folds back on to the glacis plate between the front wheels. When raised and unfolded, the trim vane is full vehicle width. It has clear panels in it so the driver has some forward vision when in the water.**

## Panhard ERC-90-F4 Armoured Car

**Country:** France
**Entered service:** 1984
**Crew:** 3
**Weight:** 8,331kg/8.2 tons
**Dimensions:** Length – 5.27m/17ft 3in
　　Height – 2.32m/7ft 7in
　　Width – 2.5m/8ft 3in
**Armament:** Main – 90mm/3.54in Model 62 F1 gun, and coaxial 7.62mm/0.3in machine-gun
　　Secondary – 7.62mm/0.3in machine-gun
**Armour:** Classified
**Powerplant:** Peugeot 6-cylinder 108kW/145hp petrol engine
**Performance:** Speed – 95kph/60mph
　　Range – 700km/435 miles

LEFT: **This M3 is taking part in an exercise. This vehicle is fitted with an STB rotary support shield, which is armed with a 7.62mm/0.3in machine-gun.** ABOVE: **The large square rear of the M3, with two large doors for the infantry section to use. The vehicle is wider in the middle than at the end and also tapers down slightly towards the middle.**

# Panhard M3 Armoured Personnel Carrier

Panhard started development of the M3 as a private venture for the export market. The first prototype was completed in 1969 and put through a series of trials. The design was subsequently changed, and in 1971 the first vehicle came off the production line. Some 1,500 M3 vehicles have been produced and exported to 26 countries and it was still in service with 12 of these countries in 2002. The M3 uses 95 per cent of the same automotive parts as the AML armoured car.

The hull of the M3 is an all-welded steel construction and gives the crew protection from small arms and shell splinters. The driver's position is on the centreline in the front of the vehicle and may be fitted with night-driving equipment. The engine compartment is behind this, with the air intake above and behind the driver. The air outlets are on either side of the roof along with one exhaust system tube per side. Behind the engine is the troop compartment with accommodation for ten men. There are

four doors in this compartment: two, both fitted with firing ports, mounted in the rear of the vehicle, and a large single door on each side of the M3. There are three firing ports down each side of the infantry compartment. Behind the engine in the roof of the vehicle is a forward hatch that can mount a wide range of turrets, cupolas and machine-gun mounts, which can in turn be armed with a variety of machine-guns and cannon. Anti-tank missiles such as MILAN can also be fitted to the M3. There is a second hatch in the rear of the roof of the troop compartment and this is normally fitted with a pintle mount for a 7.62mm/0.3in machine-gun. The M3 is fully amphibious and uses its wheels to propel itself through the water.

There are five variations on the basic vehicle; these are M3/VAT repair vehicle, M3/VPC command vehicle, M3/VLA engineering vehicle, M3/VTS ambulance and the M3 radar vehicle. In 1986 the Panhard Buffalo replaced the M3, on which it is based, in production.

ABOVE: **An M3 armed with an automatic 7.62mm/0.3in machine-gun. The vehicle has a cluster of two smoke dischargers on each side of the vehicle. The driver's hatch is open and swung out to the right of the vehicle.**

## Panhard M3 Armoured Personnel Carrier

**Country:** France
**Entered service:** 1971
**Crew:** 2 plus 10 infantry
**Weight:** 6,096kg/6 tons
**Dimensions:** Length – 4.45m/14ft 6in
   Height – 2.48m/8ft 2in
   Width – 2.4m/7ft 9in
**Armament:** Main – 7.62mm/0.3in machine-gun
   Secondary – 7.62mm/0.3in machine-gun
**Armour:** Maximum – 12mm/0.47in
**Powerplant:** Panhard 4HD 4-cylinder 67kW/90hp petrol engine
**Performance:** Speed – 100kph/62mph
   Range – 600km/372 miles

# Piranha Armoured Personnel Carrier

The MOWAG Piranha is a complete range of armoured vehicles and is available as 4x4, 6x6 and 8x8 chassis. This collection of vehicles started life as a private venture and was designed for the domestic and export market. Development started in 1972 and production started in 1976. The first customer was the Canadian Armed Forces and in February 1977 they placed an order for 350 6x6 vehicles which was very quickly increased to 491 6x6s.

The Piranha has an all-welded steel construction that protects the crew from small-arms fire and shell splinters. The driver sits at the front of the vehicle on the left-hand side and has a single-piece hatch with three periscopes in the front of it. The driver's position can also be fitted with night-driving equipment. The engine is next to the driver on the right-hand side of the vehicle with the air intake and outlet louvers on the

top of the hull. The exhaust exit is on the right-hand side of the hull. The main armament is normally turret-mounted and this is positioned behind the driver on the centreline of the vehicle.

In the rear of the vehicle is the troop compartment that usually holds 11 men, although this number can be lower depending on the type of turret fitted to the vehicle. The main exit and entry to the compartment is via two large doors that open outwards. There are two hatches in the roof of the troop compartment and, depending on the customer's requirements, firing ports can be fitted into the sides of the vehicle and in the rear doors. Steering is on the front axle for the 4x4 and 6x6 vehicles, and on the front two axles on the 8x8. The fixed rear axles have torsion-bar suspension while the axles that can steer are fitted with coil springs. All the Piranha family are fully amphibious and are propelled in the water by two propellers. Once the trim vane, which is stowed under the nose of the APC, is raised, the vehicle is ready for the water in only a few minutes. The Piranha comes with an NBC kit fitted as standard and a full air-conditioning system.

ABOVE: **This Piranha prototype is fitted with a 90mm/3.54in Cockerill Mk III gun. On the front of the turret on each side is a cluster of three smoke dischargers. The vehicle commander's and gunner's hatches are open.**
LEFT: **This Piranha is fitted with a Blazer 25 air-defence gun turret. This is fitted with 25mm/0.98in GAU-12/U cannon, and four Stinger SAMs are fitted above the gun barrel. The gun is firing and the large number of empty shells can be seen being ejected from the weapon.**

All members of the Piranha family share many of the same components such as the front and rear hull sections, doors, hatches, wheel drives, wheels, differentials, suspension, steering and propellers, which makes maintenance of the vehicles easier and cheaper. The Piranha family has been designed to fill a wide variety of roles for both the military and internal security forces, for example ambulance, anti-tank, armoured personnel carrier, command, mortar carrier, recovery and reconnaissance. The most popular version of the Piranha family is the 6x6 which can be fitted with a wide array of armaments. This includes a remote-controlled 7.62mm/0.3in machine-gun, a 12.7mm/0.5in machine-gun turret, 20mm/0.79in GAD-AOA Oerlikon turret, 25mm/0.98in GBD series turret, a 30mm/1.18in turret and a two-man turret armed with a 90mm/3.54in Cockerill or Mecar gun. The Canadians and Australians have fitted the British Scorpion 76mm/2.99in L23A1 gun turret to a number of their vehicles.

The Swiss Army had a requirement for 400 6x6 Piranha anti-tank vehicles to replace the ageing 106mm/4.17in M40 recoilless rifle in Swiss Army service. Each Swiss infantry regiment has nine of these anti-tank vehicles in a tank-destroyer company. They are armed with the Norwegian Thune-Eureka twin TOW turret, which has a hatch in the rear for the gunner. In the forward part of the turret are the sight and guidance systems and these are the same as for the basic infantry version of the TOW. Within two seconds of the first

ABOVE: **This Piranha is fitted with a remote-controlled Oerlikon 25mm/0.98in GBD-COA turret. The gunner sits inside the vehicle and can select two different types of ammunition. The driver's hatch is at the front of the vehicle with the commander's hatch behind, while the engine intake grills are to the left.**

missile impacting, the turret can lock on to another target ready to fire again. Reloading is carried out from the rear of the turret and can be completed in 40 seconds for the two missiles.

The Piranha has been built under licence in a large number of countries and has proved to be very successful, reliable and well-liked by its crews. It is expected to remain in service until 2020. In 2005, the Piranha family of vehicles was in service with 14 different countries, and a new version of the family, the Piranha IV, is currently being developed.

RIGHT: **This is a Blazer 30 air-defence system fitted to a Piranha. The turret is armed with a 30mm/1.18in cannon, while above the cannon are four Javelin SAMs. The radar is mounted to the rear of the turret on a pintle mount.**

ABOVE RIGHT: **The Piranha armed with a Belgian CM90 turret. This turret is also armed with the Cockerill 90mm/3.45in gun and has a row of seven smoke dischargers on each side of the turret.** LEFT: **This MOWAG Piranha is armed with the Italian OTO Melara Quad 25mm/0.98in AA system. The gunner sits in the middle of the turret, with his hatch opening to the rear. The turret can complete a full traverse in just three seconds.**

## Piranha 6x6 APC

**Country:** Switzerland
**Entered service:** 1977
**Crew:** 3 plus 11 infantry
**Weight:** 10,465kg/10.3 tons
**Dimensions:** Length – 5.97m/19ft 6in
Height – 1.85m/6ft 1in
Width – 2.5m/8ft 2in
**Armament:** Main – Variable
Secondary – Small arms
**Armour:** Maximum – 10mm/0.394in
**Powerplant:** GM Detroit Diesel 6V-53T 6-cylinder 261kW/350hp diesel engine
**Performance:** Speed – 100kph/62mph
Range – 600km/370 miles

LEFT: **The trim vane of the vehicle is folded back against the glacis plate. In the front of the hull are the headlights, and the commander's cupola is fitted with a 7.62mm/0.3in machine-gun. On each side of the turret is a row of four smoke dischargers.**
ABOVE: **This Luchs is negotiating a German driver-training course. The suspension is operating in several directions on all the wheels of the vehicle. The searchlight on the left-hand side of the turret is covered. The Luchs has developed a very good reputation for its cross-country ability.**

# Radspahpanzer Luchs Reconnaissance Vehicle

In 1964, the Federal German Army issued a requirement for a new family of vehicles, including an 8x8 armoured amphibious reconnaissance vehicle, to enter service in the 1970s. The prototypes were delivered for testing in 1968 and in 1971, the Daimler-Benz candidate was chosen, with a contract for 408 vehicles being placed in 1973. The first production vehicles were completed in May 1975 and the first vehicle was handed over to the army in September 1975. In service it is known as by the German Army as the Luchs. Production continued until 1978.

The hull of the Luchs is an all-welded steel construction which gives the crew protection from small-arms fire and shell splinters, while the front of the vehicle is proof against 2cm/0.79in cannon fire.

The driver is located in the front of the Luchs on the left-hand side and this position can be fitted with night-driving equipment. The two-man Rheinmetall TS-7 turret is situated to the rear of the driver, with the commander stationed on the right-hand side and the gunner on the left. This turret is fitted with spaced armour to improve protection. A searchlight is fitted to the left-hand side of the turret and is connected to the elevation controls of the gun. This can also be used in the infrared mode. Both the commander and the gunner are equipped with sights for the main gun.

The fourth man in the crew is the radio operator/rear driver, and they are seated behind the turret facing the rear of the vehicle on the left-hand side with the engine compartment on the right.

There is a large hatch that gives access to all crew positions in the left-hand side of the hull between the front four and rear four wheels. The Luchs is fully amphibious and is propelled through the water by two propellers mounted at the rear of the vehicle. Steering is on the front and rear axles which makes this vehicle very manoeuvrable.

The Luchs has developed a very good reputation for its cross-country ability, reliability and quietness.

LEFT: **A Luchs leaving the water with its trim vane in the raised position. To give the driver some forward vision when in the water, the trim vane has several clear panels fitted in it.**

## Radspahpanzer Luchs Reconnaissance Vehicle

**Country:** West Germany
**Entered service:** 1975
**Crew:** 4
**Weight:** 19,507kg/19.2 tons
**Dimensions:** Length – 7.74m/25ft 5in
  Height – 2.9m/9ft 6in
  Width – 2.98m/9ft 9in
**Armament:** Main – 2cm/0.79in MK20 Rh202
  cannon
  Secondary – 1 x 7.62mm/0.3in MG3
  machine-gun
**Armour:** Classified
**Powerplant:** Daimler-Benz OM 403A 10-cylinder
  291kW/390hp diesel engine
**Performance:** Speed – 90kph/56mph
  Range – 730km/455 miles

# Rapier Tracked SAM Vehicle

LEFT: **A Rapier Tracked SAM Vehicle that has just launched a missile. The tracking radar on the rear of the turret can be seen in the raised position. The vehicle is divided into two clear parts: the crew and engine compartment to the front and the missile launcher/radar to the rear.**

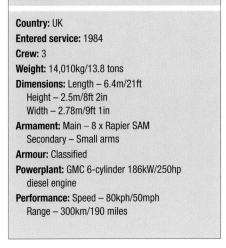

### Rapier Tracked SAM Vehicle

**Country:** UK
**Entered service:** 1984
**Crew:** 3
**Weight:** 14,010kg/13.8 tons
**Dimensions:** Length – 6.4m/21ft
  Height – 2.5m/8ft 2in
  Width – 2.78m/9ft 1in
**Armament:** Main – 8 x Rapier SAM
  Secondary – Small arms
**Armour:** Classified
**Powerplant:** GMC 6-cylinder 186kW/250hp
  diesel engine
**Performance:** Speed – 80kph/50mph
  Range – 300km/190 miles

Development of this vehicle commenced in 1974, initially using the chassis of the M548, but this was quickly changed for the RCM 748, part of the M113 APC family of vehicles. Originally developed for the Imperial Iranian Armed Forces, British Aerospace was left with a number of these vehicles and no customer following the overthrow of the Shah in 1979. Subsequently, the British Army agreed to conduct vehicle trials and in 1981 placed an order for 50 units. It entered service in 1984 with two Royal Artillery Regiments, each deploying 24 Rapier vehicles.

The hull is an all-welded aluminium construction, and is proof against small-arms fire and shell splinters. The driver, commander and gunner all share the very small and cramped cab in the front of the vehicle. The driver is on the left-hand side, while the engine is installed behind the crew compartment. The eight-round Rapier system is mounted on the rear of the vehicle. The time taken from the vehicle stopping to the first target being engaged is 15 seconds.

# Rooikat 105mm Armoured Car

Development on this vehicle started in 1978. The first production vehicles were completed in 1989 and entered service in 1990, armed with a 76mm/2.99in fully stabilized gun.

### Rooikat 105mm Armoured Car

**Country:** South Africa
**Entered service:** 1994
**Crew:** 4
**Weight:** 28,042kg/27.6 tons
**Dimensions:** Length – 7.09m/23ft 3in
  Height – 2.8m/9ft 2in
  Width – 2.9m/9ft 6in
**Armament:** Main – 105mm/4.13in GT7 gun,
  and coaxial 7.62mm/0.3in machine-gun
  Secondary –1 x 7.62mm/0.3in machine-gun
**Armour:** Classified
**Powerplant:** 10-cylinder 420kW/563hp
  diesel engine
**Performance:** Speed – 120kph/75mph
  Range – 1,000km/620 miles

In 1994, further development resulted in a 105mm/4.13in version of the vehicle entering service with the South African National Defence Force. Total production so far has been 240 vehicles.

The hull is an all-welded steel construction, and is proof against small-arms fire, shell splinters and anti-tank mines. The front of the vehicle is proof against 24mm/0.94in cannon fire. The driver's position is located in the front on the centreline, while the other three members of the crew are situated in the turret. The commander and gunner are on the right-hand side of the turret with the loader on the left. The engine is in the rear of the vehicle, which can be driven in either 8x4 mode or 8x8 mode

ABOVE: **The turret of this Rooikat is fitted with two clusters of four smoke dischargers on each side and the barrel is locked in the travel cradle. The wiper blade fitted to the driver's visor can also be clearly seen.**

and accelerate from 0–30kph/0–18.6mph in under eight seconds.

The Rooikat is designed for the reconnaissance role but can also carry out "seek and destroy" missions.

# SA-8b SAM Vehicle

The SA-8 has the NATO designation "Gecko" and is an all-weather low-altitude Surface-to-Air Missile (SAM) system. The Gecko entered service in 1974 with the Soviet Armed Forces and was seen for the first time at the November Parade in Moscow in 1975. It was designed to fill the gap between the SA-7/SA-9 and the SA-6 and was developed in conjunction with the Soviet Navy SA-N-4 system. The Gecko is known in the Russian Army as the ZRK-SD Romb (*Zentniy Raketniy Komplex*) which indicates that the system is a complete SAM system. Each anti-aircraft division has 20 of these vehicles. This was the first anti-aircraft system to combine the surveillance, target-acquisition and missile launcher all-in-one vehicle.

The chassis of the Gecko, an all-welded steel construction, is based on the ZIL-167 6x6 truck and is not proof against small arms or shell splinters. The crew compartment is at the front of the vehicle where all three crew members sit in a row with the driver in the centre. In the roof above the driver is a small hatch which is the only access to and from the vehicle. The main missile control consoles, operated by all three crew members, are behind the crew. The vehicle is very spacious and the crew can even sleep in it. The engine is in the rear of the vehicle with the air intakes and outlets built into the top of the hull, while the exhaust is at the rear of the engine compartment.

The central radar dish is the main tracking system with the two smaller dishes acting as target-acquisition radar. On the top of the radar mount is a television camera which is used to acquire targets without having to switch on the radar. The SA-8b variant can carry

ABOVE LEFT: **The boat-shaped hull of the vehicle can be clearly seen, with the trim vane folded back in front of the windscreen. The missile turret sits high on the top of the vehicle.** ABOVE: **The main entry and exit hatch for the crew of the Gecko is in the roof of the vehicle immediately in front of the main radar dish and is seen here in the open position.**

six missiles (the SA-8a carries only four) and no reloads. The Gecko is fully amphibious, propelled in the water by two water jets built into the rear of the vehicle, and is also air-transportable. The vehicle has been used in combat and is very popular with several armies in the Middle East.

LEFT: **The main search radar of the Gecko is in the travel mode; it is folded down against the missile launching boxes. The water jet entry hatch is sited above the rear wheel with the exit in the rear of the vehicle.**

## SA-8b SAM Vehicle

**Country:** USSR
**Entered service:** 1974
**Crew:** 3
**Weight:** 17,499kg/17.2 tons
**Dimensions:** Length – 9.14m/30ft
  Height – 4.2m/13ft 10in
  Width – 2.8m/9ft 2in
**Armament:** Main – 6 x SA-8b missiles
  Secondary – Small arms
**Armour:** Classified
**Powerplant:** 5D20 B-300 223kW/299hp
  diesel engine
**Performance:** Speed – 80kph/50mph
  Range – 250km/155 miles

LEFT: **This Saladin armoured car has a machine-gun mounted in front of the commander's position. The external storage boxes can be seen mounted on the top of the wheels.**

BELOW: **A Saladin of the 3rd Royal Tank Regiment in Malaya. Behind are two Ferret armoured cars. The Saladin is covered in personal kit, which in combat was stored on the outside of the vehicle.**

# Saladin Mk 2 Armoured Car

In 1947, a contract was issued to Alvis Ltd to develop a new 6x6 armoured car for the British Army. A mock-up was completed in 1948 and was given the designation of FV 601. This first vehicle was to be armed with a 2pdr gun (FV 601A) but this was quickly dropped in favour of a 76mm/2.99in gun (FV 601B). The first prototype vehicles were delivered in 1952–53 and were followed by six pre-production vehicles. Further modifications were made to these vehicles as a result of trials, in particular the turret was redesigned. In 1958 the FV 601C or Saladin Mk 2 entered production with the first vehicles being completed in 1959 and entering service the same year. Production continued until 1972, by which time 1,177 Saladins had been built.

The hull and turret of the vehicle were all-welded steel constructions and were proof against small-arms fire and shell splinters. The driver was located in the front of the vehicle on the centreline with a hatch in front that folded down on to the glacis plate. There was powered steering to the four front wheels. The steering wheel was rather oddly fitted sloping into the driver's chest, which took some getting used to. Behind and above the driver was the turret which housed the other two members of the crew. The commander was on the right-hand side of the turret with the gunner on the left. Both had hatches in the roof of the turret and the commander had a pintle mount for a 7.62mm/0.3in machine-gun. There was an escape hatch for the crew

below the turret in each side of the hull, while the engine and three fuel tanks were in the rear of the vehicle. The Saladin was not fitted with any form of NBC system, and did not carry night-driving or night-fighting equipment.

The CVR(T) 76mm/2.99in Scorpion replaced the Saladin in British Army service. Saladins would see service in many parts of the world, their last combat operation being in defence of Kuwait City during the 1991 Gulf War when they destroyed several T-55 MBTs.

| Saladin Mk 2 Armoured Car | |
|---|---|
| **Country:** UK | |
| **Entered service:** 1959 | |
| **Crew:** 3 | |
| **Weight:** 11,582kg/11.4 tons | |
| **Dimensions:** Length – 4.92m/16ft 2in<br>    Height – 2.92m/8ft 7in<br>    Width – 2.53m/8ft 4in | |
| **Armament:** Main – 76mm/2.99in L5A1 gun,<br>    and coaxial 7.62mm/0.3in machine-gun<br>    Secondary – 7.62mm/0.3in machine-gun | |
| **Armour:** Maximum – 16mm/0.63in | |
| **Powerplant:** Rolls-Royce B80 Mk 6A 8-cylinder<br>    127kW/170hp petrol engine | |
| **Performance:** Speed – 72kph/45mph<br>    Range – 400km/250 miles | |

RIGHT: **A detail of the front of a Saladin. On each side of the front of the turret are two clusters of six smoke dischargers. The driver's hatch has been pushed open; this makes a very useful shelf for a mug of tea.**

LEFT: **A Saracen command vehicle. The tube frame on the rear of the vehicle is for a tent extension to be fitted to increase the working space. This vehicle has been fitted with a turret with a cluster of four smoke dischargers on each side on the top of the vehicle,** BELOW: **This vehicle has a light machine-gun fitted to the ring mount that is set in the rear of the roof. Most of the vision ports are in the open position; these are not fitted with any form of glass. A fire extinguisher is fitted to the rear mudguard of the Saracen, while camouflage netting has been stored above the centre road wheel.**

# Saracen Armoured Personnel Carrier

After World War II, the British Army issued a requirement for a family of vehicles that were all 6x6 configurations. These were given the family designation FV 600. The family was made up of the FV 601 Saladin Armoured Car, the FV 602 Command Vehicle (which was cancelled but was later reincarnated as the FV 604) and the FV 603 Saracen Armoured Personnel Carrier. Development of the Saracen started in 1948 with the first prototype completed in 1952. The first production vehicle was completed in December 1952 and the type entered service in early 1953. The Saracen was rushed into production and given priority over the other vehicles in the family as a result of the emergency in Malaya. The Saracen would remain the main APC of the British Army throughout the 1950s and 1960s until replaced by the FV 432. Production continued until 1972, by which time 1,838 vehicles had been produced. Some of these vehicles are still in service with a few armed forces around the world. All vehicles in the family would share many of the same automotive parts and the unusual steering-wheel angle (see the Saladin). The last vehicle in the family was the Stalwart Amphibious Load Carrier (FV 620).

The hull of the Saracen is an all-welded steel construction, and is proof against small-arms fire and shell splinters. The radiator is in the front of the vehicle with the engine behind. The crew and troop compartments are all one in this vehicle, with the driver's position situated on the centreline in the front of the compartment directly behind the engine. There is no windscreen; the driver looks through a hatch that folds down and lays on the top of the engine in non-combat situations. The troop commander sits behind the driver facing forwards on the left-hand side of the vehicle, and also doubles as vehicle commander. The radio operator sits behind the driver on the right-hand side of the vehicle and also faces forwards. Between the commander and the radio operator is the machine-gun turret position. This is the same type of turret as that fitted to the Ferret Mk 2 armoured car and is un-powered.

LEFT: **This aerial view shows the front turret and the rear ring mount on the roof of the Saracen APC. The turret is fitted with a searchlight on the left-hand side, while two fixed steps at the rear make boarding quicker for the infantry.**

LEFT: **This Saracen has all the vision ports in the open position and the driver's hatch is in the half-open position. The Saracen has a cluster of three smoke dischargers on each front mudguard. The headlights proved to be very vulnerable to damage.**
ABOVE: **A Saracen on exercise in Britain. The driver has his hatch in the open position, while the vehicle commander is talking into the radio. The Saracen can continue to operate with a damaged wheel on each side of the vehicle.**

In the rear of the compartment is accommodation for eight troops, who sit four down each side facing inwards. There are two large doors in the rear of the vehicle, each of which has a firing port. These are the main entrance and exit from the vehicle for the crew and the troops. Below the doors are two steps and between them is a large towing hitch. In the rear of the roof behind the turret is a large sliding hatch which gives access to a ring-mounted anti-aircraft machine-gun which was initially an LMG, better known as the World War II Bren gun. Subsequently, this was replaced by a 7.62mm/0.3in machine-gun. There are also three firing ports in each side of the vehicle. The Saracen has no NBC system, night-driving or night-fighting equipment and is not amphibious, but can ford shallow water. Along with the other vehicles in the family, the Saracen can continue to operate on the battlefield even if it loses two wheels as a result of mine explosions, provided the wheels are lost one from each side.

The FV 603C was a tropical version of the Saracen. These were built mainly for Kuwait and had reverse-flow cooling. The air was sucked in at the rear of the engine, passed over the

engine and out through the radiator. Libya also placed an order for these vehicles but they were never delivered due to the political situation, the Libyan vehicles being taken over by the British Army and sent to Northern Ireland. The FV 604 Command Vehicle was modified for the command role and had a crew of six, with map-boards and extra radios inside. The FV 610 was another command vehicle but was taller and wider than the FV 604 and saw service with the British Army in Northern Ireland. The FV 610 could also be fitted with FACE (Field Artillery Computer Equipment) and was trialled with the Robert Radar System but this progressed no further than a trials vehicle. The FV 611 was the ambulance version of the Saracen and could accommodate ten walking-wounded or three stretcher cases and medical personnel. Some of these vehicles remain in service around the world to this day.

BELOW: **This Saracen command vehicle has been fitted with an additional layer of armour. The cut-out around the driver's visors can be seen. The ring mount from the rear of the roof has been moved forward for the vehicle commander, as the turret has been removed.**

## Saracen Armoured Personnel Carrier

**Country:** UK
**Entered service:** 1953
**Crew:** 2 plus 10 infantry
**Weight:** 10,160kg/10 tons
**Dimensions:** Length – 5.23m/17ft 2in
    Height – 2.46m/8ft 1in
    Width – 2.53m/8ft 4in
**Armament:** Main – 7.62mm/0.3in machine-gun
    Secondary – 7.62mm/0.3in machine-gun
**Armour:** Maximum – 16mm/0.63in
**Powerplant:** Rolls-Royce B80 Mk 6A 8-cylinder
    127kW/170hp petrol engine
**Performance:** Speed – 72kph/45mph
    Range – 400km/250 miles

LEFT: **The vehicle commander is in his turret. Note the prominent engine grills and the large single door in front of the storage boxes on the side of the vehicle. The driver's vision blocks are bullet-proof and provide a good view from his position high up in the front of the vehicle.**

# Saxon Armoured Personnel Carrier

In 1970, GKN Sankey started a private venture development of a wheeled personnel carrier for use in the internal security role. The development vehicle was known as the AT 104. It had the engine mounted at the front of the vehicle similar to the Saracen and although the armour around the engine was poor, the floor of the vehicle was redesigned to give better anti-mine protection. The first prototype vehicle of an improved design was produced in 1974, entering production in 1976 for the export market only with the designation AT 105. The name "Saxon" was not given to the vehicle officially until 1982. After further development, production would start for the British Army in 1983 and the Saxon entered service in 1984. Over 800 of these vehicles have been produced, with some 600 serving with the British Army.

The hull of the Saxon is an all-welded steel construction that gives the crew protection from small-arms fire and shell splinters. The floor of the vehicle is V-shaped, giving the crew and troops inside some protection from mines. The axles, however, are not protected. The chassis and automotive parts are taken from the Bedford MK design and these standard parts make logistics easier. However, to remove the engine the roof of the vehicle needs to be taken off which is time-consuming, requires heavy equipment, and makes maintenance in the field difficult.

The Saxon can be built in left- and right-hand drive versions. The driver's compartment is in the front of the vehicle on either the left- or right-hand side as required and can be accessed from the main troop compartment or from a large single hatch

RIGHT: **A convoy of three Saxon APCs on exercise with the vehicle commanders positioned in their turrets. Wire-mesh storage baskets are installed on the roof of each vehicle and a spare wheel is carried under the side door on the right-hand side.**

in the roof of the driving compartment. The driver has three large bullet-proof vision blocks, one to the front and one in each side. The engine compartment is next to the driver, on either the right or the left of the vehicle depending on the configuration. The radiator grill is mounted in the front of the vehicle with the air outlet on the side of the vehicle, and again this is installed on one side or the other depending on the driving position.

Behind and above the driver's position is the vehicle commander's fixed cupola which is a four-sided box with all-round vision blocks and a large single hatch in the roof. There are machine-gun pintle mounts on each side of the cupola for a single 7.62mm/0.3in GPMG. As this cupola is only bolted to the roof of the vehicle, it can be replaced very quickly with a manually traversed machine-gun turret which can be armed with a single or twin 7.62mm/0.3in machine-gun. Alongside the commander's position in the hull of the vehicle is a single large door which in British service is normally fitted on the right-hand side of the vehicle, but again this door can be moved to the other side of the vehicle or two side doors can be fitted as required. The main troop compartment holds eight men, four down each side of the vehicle facing inwards. In the rear of the Saxon are two large doors that are the main exit and entrance for the infantry section using the vehicle. Each door is fitted with both a vision block and a firing port and there is another firing port in the front of the vehicle next to the driver. The British Army has fitted large storage boxes to the sides of the vehicle and a mesh rack to the roof behind the commander's cupola to improve personal equipment storage.

The Saxon recovery vehicle, designed to recover vehicles of its own type and soft-skin trucks, has been in service with the British Army for many years. This has a crew of four and a 5,080kg/5-ton hydraulic winch mounted on the left-hand side of the vehicle. A tent can be fitted to the vehicle to act as a covered workshop. In 2005, the Saxon was undergoing an upgrade programme and a Cummins diesel engine was being substituted for the original Bedford diesel engine. A command vehicle has also been developed for the British Army and the Royal Air Force for use with the Rapier missile batteries.

ABOVE: **This is a British Army Saxon recovery vehicle, which is fitted with a 5,080kg/5-ton hydraulic winch. The large side-mounted hull door was removed from these vehicles to allow for increased equipment storage.**

ABOVE: **The headlights of the Saxon are built into the front of the vehicle to give them better protection. The high ground-clearance of the body of the vehicle, which gives the infantry inside the Saxon some protection from land mines, can be clearly seen.** BELOW: **The turret of this Saxon has been fitted with a 7.62mm/0.3in GPMG. A hessian screen, which is rolled down when the vehicle is parked to help camouflage it, has been attached to the lower hull of the Saxon. The driver's hatch is open and folded forward. The spare wheel can be clearly seen attached to the underside of the vehicle.**

## Saxon Armoured Personnel Carrier

**Country:** UK
**Entered service:** 1984
**Crew:** 2 plus 8 infantry
**Weight:** 11,684kg/11.5 tons
**Dimensions:** Length – 5.17m/17ft
Height – 2.63m/8ft 7in
Width – 2.49m/8ft 2in
**Armament:** Main – 7.62mm/0.3in GPMG
Secondary – Small arms
**Armour:** Classified
**Powerplant:** Cummins 6BT 6-cylinder
122kW/160hp diesel engine
**Performance:** Speed – 96kph/60mph
Range – 510km/317 miles

# Scud Missile System TEL

The Scud missile system was developed in response to the Soviet Army's requirement in the early 1950s for a tactical missile system that could deliver both conventional and nuclear warheads. This was to replace the Soviet-developed R-1 and R-2 missiles, which were based on the German V2 ballistic missile. These battery systems required 152 trucks, 70 trailers and over 500 men and could only fire 9 missiles per day. The new missile was called the R-11 (NATO codename Scud A). Its first test flight was in April 1953 and production began in 1955. The first TEL (Tractor, Erector and Launcher) was developed using the ISU-152 (Obiekt 218) tank chassis. These TEL vehicles, known as 8U218, entered service with the Soviet forces in 1955. They were deployed at the density of one regiment per army; each regiment being composed of three batteries, each of which had three TEL vehicles. These 9 TEL vehicles were supported by 200 trucks and 1,200 personnel and had an allocation of 27 missiles per day. It is believed that 100 TEL vehicles were built for the Soviet Army. In 1960 Khrushchev ordered that Soviet heavy tank production should be stopped and the decision was taken to develop a new TEL.

This new vehicle was based on the MAZ-543LTM 8x8 heavy truck, a standard Soviet heavy truck design. The wheeled chassis has many advantages over the tracked chassis. It provides a smoother ride which causes less vibration damage to the missile and the control and test equipment on the vehicle, and is a more reliable and cost-effective vehicle, with only a slight decrease in cross-country performance compared to the tracked chassis. The vehicle has a full set of power-assisted controls for the steering and gearbox which makes it easy to drive. All the wheels are connected to a central tyre pressure system that is regulated from the driver's position.

The vehicle was given the official designation of 9P117 TEL and the official name of "Uragan" (Hurricane) but was

TOP: **A Soviet Scud missile TEL about to take part in a November Parade. The compartment between the second and third wheels is the main fire control centre. The compartment on the other side of the vehicle holds the auxiliary power unit.** ABOVE: **A Soviet Scud B is halfway up to the vertical firing position, while the Scud behind is in the firing position. The six-man launch crew is attaching the control cables to the missile as it is being raised.**

popularly known as the "Kashalot" (Sperm Whale) by the Soviet Army because of its size. The driver is situated in the front of the left-hand crew compartment and has a very simple set of controls. Behind the driver is a member of the launch crew with a set of compressed air bottles between them which

supply the power for the cold weather starter. The other crew compartment on the right side of the vehicle has the vehicle commander, the main communications equipment and the fourth crew member in it. Between the two crew compartments is the radiator and main engine, which is not shielded and can betray the vehicle's position with its heat signature. The exhaust from this comes out between the first and second wheels. Behind the crew cabins is an APU that is used when the main engine is shut down.

The missile and its erector are carried in a cavity down the centre of the vehicle when in the travelling mode. In the centre of the vehicle are two control cabins. The left-hand cabin houses the main selector switches and an auxiliary power unit. The right-hand cabin has accommodation for the targeting controls and missile testing equipment, along with seats for two crew members. The vehicle carries its own launching base-plate which is hydraulically operated and is folded up against the rear of the vehicle when in the travelling mode. Between this base-plate and the vehicle are two large stabilizing jacks that help support the weight of the missile when it is in the erect position. On the left-hand side at the rear of the vehicle is the main safety catch for the missile; this is a simple mechanical slide that is moved under the fuel pump switches.

The Scud B was first used in action during the war between Egypt and Israel in 1973. The next major use of the system was between 1986 and 1988 during the "War of the Cities" between Iran and Iraq. Long-range versions of the Scud were fired against Israel and Saudi Arabia during the 1991 Gulf War, but the largest number of missiles was fired by the Soviets during the Afghan War (1979–89) when 1,000 were fired against mountain villages.

TOP: **The two separate crew compartments with the radiator and missile warhead between them can be clearly seen. The driver's cab is on the left-hand side of the vehicle, while in the rear of the cab are a crew member and the compressed-air starting system for the vehicle.** ABOVE: **On the rear of the vehicle are two hydraulic jacks that are lowered into position before the missile is raised. The firing platform swings down with the missile resting on it. There are access ladders on the arms of the cradle.** MIDDLE LEFT: **A Scud TEL taking part in a parade. The front four wheels are used for steering the vehicle, with the exhaust system exiting between the first and second wheels. The large clamp just behind the warhead attaches the missile to the TEL.**

LEFT: **The red dot on the vehicle is a heavy canvas security blind covering the little window in the control cabin. The small ladder above the third wheel swings down to give access to the top of the TEL.**

## MAZ 9P117 TEL

**Country:** USSR
**Entered service:** 1965
**Crew:** 4
**Weight:** 37,400kg/36.4 tons
**Dimensions:** Length – 13.36m/43ft 9in
Height – 3.33m/10ft 10in
Width – 3.02m/9ft 10in
**Armament:** Main – R300 missile
Secondary – None
**Armour:** None
**Powerplant:** D12A-525A 12-cylinder 391kW/525hp diesel engine
**Performance:** Speed – 45kph/28mph
Range – 450km/280 miles

# Spartan Armoured Personnel Carrier

The Spartan was a development of the Scorpion CVR(T) and entered service with the British Army in 1978. It was designed to perform in a number of roles that the Saracen 6x6 APC had previously filled, but was not designed as a direct replacement for the FV 432 APC. Subsequently, this very adaptable vehicle has been deployed as a carrier for the Royal Artillery Blowpipe/Javelin surface-to-air missile teams, as a missile reload vehicle for the Striker and as a carrier for Royal Engineer assault teams. By 2001, 960 Spartan vehicles had been built. The late production vehicles have an improved suspension and a new fuel-efficient Cummins diesel engine fitted, and a large number of the early production vehicles have also now had these improvements fitted.

While officially the Spartan is designated as an APC, it can only carry four men in the rear of the vehicle. Its hull is an all-welded aluminium construction which is proof against small-arms fire and shell splinters. The driver is located in the front of the vehicle on the left-hand side and has a wide-angle periscope which can be replaced by passive night-driving equipment. Next to the driver on the right-hand side is the Jaguar 4.2-litre petrol engine, with air intakes and outlets on the glacis plate while the exhaust is on the roof on the right-hand side. The vehicle commander/gunner is behind the driver and is provided with a cupola mounted in the vehicle roof with eight periscopes, which provide all-round vision. Mounted on the right of the cupola is a 7.62mm/0.3in machine-gun

ABOVE LEFT: **A Spartan fitted with the Euromissile MILAN MCT turret. The launcher rails are empty on this vehicle. The long sloping glacis plate can clearly be seen.** ABOVE: **This Spartan has both the driver's and commander's hatches open. The driver's hatch opens towards the front of the vehicle. The Spartan has two clusters of three smoke dischargers fitted to the glacis plate.**

which can be aimed and fired from inside the vehicle. Next to the commander on the right of the vehicle is the troop commander/radio operator, who also has a hatch in the roof. In the rear of the vehicle is the troop compartment which holds four men, one seated behind the troop commander and three others on a bench seat on the left-hand side. Entry and exit from the vehicle is via a large single door in the rear.

ABOVE: **A group of soldiers loading their sleeping bags into the back of the Spartan. The commander's cupola has its hatch in the open position.**

## Spartan APC

**Country:** UK
**Entered service:** 1978
**Crew:** 2 plus 5 infantry
**Weight:** 8,128kg/8 tons
**Dimensions:** Length – 5.13m/16ft 11in
　　　Height – 2.26m/7ft 5in
　　　Width – 2.24m/7ft 4in
**Armament:** Main – 7.62mm/0.3in machine-gun
　　　Secondary – Small arms
**Armour:** Classified
**Powerplant:** Jaguar J60 No.1 Mk 100B 6-cylinder
　　　142kW/190hp petrol engine
**Performance:** Speed – 80kph/50mph
　　　Range – 483km/301 miles

LEFT: **An infantry section debussing from a Stormer IFV. The vehicle is armed with a Helio FVT 900 turret which is fitted with a 20mm/0.79in cannon. In the hull of the vehicle are firing ports for the infantry to use from inside the vehicle.** BELOW: **A Stormer fitted with a two-man turret, armed with a 30mm/1.18in cannon and coaxial 7.62mm/0.3in machine-gun. The vehicle can carry 165 rounds of ammunition for the main gun.**

# Stormer Armoured Personnel Carrier

Development of the FV 4333 started at the Military Vehicle and Engineering Establishment in the 1970s and the first prototype was displayed in 1978. Alvis took over the development of the vehicle in June 1981, giving it the name "Stormer" and making it part of the CVR(T) family, as it uses many of the same automotive parts as the other members of this group. The Stormer is actually a stretched version of the Spartan with increased chassis length and an extra road wheel. Production began in 1982, for export orders only at first, with the first vehicles entering service with the Malaysian armed forces in 1983. In 1986 the British Army selected the Stormer for three roles: the Shielder anti-tank mine dispenser vehicle; a launch vehicle for the Starstreak SAM high-velocity missile

which entered service in 1989; and a reconnaissance vehicle for the Starstreak. Alvis have also produced a number of variations on the basic Stormer chassis but as yet none has been placed in production.

The hull of the Stormer is an all-welded aluminium construction and is proof against small-arms fire and shell splinters. The driver is located in the front of the vehicle on the left-hand side and has a single wide-angle periscope that can be replaced by passive night-driving equipment. The engine compartment is located next to the driver on the right. Behind the driver is the vehicle commander/gunner's position, which has a cupola in the roof with eight periscopes providing all-round vision and also mounts a 7.62mm/0.3in machine-gun. The radio operator/troop

commander's position is next to the vehicle commander, and behind this is the crew compartment, which accommodates eight infantry, four down each side on bench seats facing inwards. The main access point, a single large door with a vision block, is at the rear of the vehicle.

The Stormer and other members of the CVR family have a full NBC system and are air-portable. They can ford water to a depth of 1.1m/3ft 7in in their normal combat mode but, with a little preparation and the raising of a flotation screen, they become fully amphibious, propelling themselves in the water with their tracks.

LEFT: **A Stormer air defence vehicle armed with the Starstreak SAM system. The missiles are stored in their launch boxes, each box holding four missiles. A full reload is carried inside the vehicle. The flotation screen can be seen in its stored position around the edge of the vehicle.**

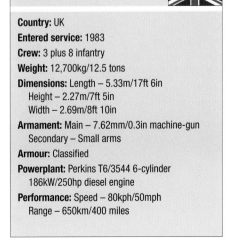

| Stormer APC | |
|---|---|
| **Country:** UK | |
| **Entered service:** 1983 | |
| **Crew:** 3 plus 8 infantry | |
| **Weight:** 12,700kg/12.5 tons | |
| **Dimensions:** Length – 5.33m/17ft 6in | |
| Height – 2.27m/7ft 5in | |
| Width – 2.69m/8ft 10in | |
| **Armament:** Main – 7.62mm/0.3in machine-gun | |
| Secondary – Small arms | |
| **Armour:** Classified | |
| **Powerplant:** Perkins T6/3544 6-cylinder | |
| 186kW/250hp diesel engine | |
| **Performance:** Speed – 80kph/50mph | |
| Range – 650km/400 miles | |

LEFT: **A Striker on a live-firing exercise. This vehicle has just launched one of the five Swingfire AT missiles that are carried in the launcher at the rear of the vehicle. The back-blast generated by the Swingfire on launching is small and so does not give away the position of the vehicle.**

BELOW: **The driver of this Striker is in his position with his hatch lying on the glacis plate. The exhaust system runs back down the right-hand side of the vehicle. At the end of the protective cover, the exhaust turns through 90 degrees and goes straight up for about 31cm/12in.**

# Striker Self-Propelled Anti-Tank Guided Weapon Vehicle

The Striker (FV 102) is part of the Scorpion CVR(T) family. The first production vehicles entered service with the British Army in 1975. The Striker uses many of the same automotive parts as the other members of the CVR family and has been designed to be an air-portable anti-tank missile system capable of destroying MBTs. Having a similar performance to the Scorpion, the Striker can move in and out of unprepared positions very quickly and is well suited to "shoot and scoot" missions. During their service careers, both the Striker vehicle and the Swingfire missile system have been upgraded but are now being phased out, as the "Spartan" vehicles, armed with the

MILAN anti-tank guided missile, are entering service with the British Army.

The hull of the Striker is an all-welded aluminium construction, and is proof against small-arms fire and shell splinters. The driver is located in the front of the vehicle on the left-hand side, with the engine next to him on the right of the vehicle. The commander/gunner is situated behind the driver, and has a cupola above his position that has all-round vision and is armed with a 7.62mm/0.3in machine-gun. Next to the vehicle commander is the guided-weapons controller. He has a sight mounted above his position – as the Swingfire is a wire-guided system – the controller has to follow the flight of the missile, which can be guided on to the target by using a joystick. The missile system can operate either in daylight or in night-time conditions and can be fired from

inside or outside the vehicle. Behind the vehicle commander's cupola is a box structure holding five ready-to-use Swingfire missiles. To bring it into the firing position the box front is elevated to 35 degrees from the horizontal. Five further missiles, accessed through a large single door, are carried in the rear of the vehicle. Reloading is performed outside the vehicle.

The Striker is capable of fording 1.1m/3ft 7in of water without preparation, but the vehicle becomes fully amphibious by fitting a flotation screen, using its tracks to propel itself through the water.

LEFT: **On the front of the Striker are two clusters of three smoke dischargers. The headlights are attached to the front of the vehicle by simple brackets.**

## Striker SP ATGW Vehicle 🇬🇧

**Country:** UK
**Entered service:** 1975
**Crew:** 3
**Weight:** 8,331kg/8.2 tons
**Dimensions:** Length – 4.83m/15ft 10in
    Height – 2.28m/7ft 6in
    Width – 2.28m/7ft 6in
**Armament:** Main – 10 x Swingfire Wire-Guided Missiles
    Secondary – 7.62mm/0.3in machine-gun
**Armour:** Classified
**Powerplant:** Jaguar J60 No.1 Mk 100B 6-cylinder 142kW/190hp
**Performance:** Speed – 80kph/50mph
    Range – 483km/301 miles

LEFT: **Two of the driver's vision blocks have been covered to protect the vision port. The turret on the roof of the vehicle is a Creusot-Loire TLI 127, and is armed with a 12.7mm/0.5in heavy machine-gun and a coaxial 7.62/0.3in machine-gun.**
ABOVE: **A Belgian BDX APC used by the air force for airfield defence. A 7.62mm/ 0.3in machine-gun is mounted on the top of the shield on the vehicle roof. Just in front of the turret on each side of the hull is a bank of three smoke dischargers.**

# Timoney Armoured Personnel Carrier

Due to the troubles in Northern Ireland, the Government of the Irish Republic decided to expand the army in the early 1970s, aiming for between 100 and 200 APC vehicles. In 1972 the Irish Army issued a requirement for a 4x4 armoured personnel carrier that could be used anywhere in the world operating under United Nations control. The Timoney brothers came up with a design, producing the first prototype in 1973. There were a large number of technical faults with this prototype vehicle, which were rectified to produce the Mk II in April 1974, and this was then put on trial with the Irish Army. After further improvements to the basic design, the Mk III was produced in 1976. Further development produced the Mk IV, of which only five vehicles were built. The final vehicle produced by Timoney in the series was the Mk VI, but again only five units were ever manufactured.

The hull of the Mk V was an all-welded steel construction, which was proof against small-arms fire and shell splinters. The vehicle could also withstand the blast from a 9kg/20lb mine. The driver was positioned in the front of the vehicle on the centreline, and had a windscreen to the front and one to each side. There were three doors in the vehicle, one in each side and one in the rear. The engine compartment was to the rear of the driver with the air louvers in the roof. There was a manual machine-gun turret armed with a single 7.62mm/0.3in machine-gun in the centre of the roof. The troop compartment in the rear had seats for ten men. The vehicle was fully amphibious, propelling itself through the water using its wheels.

The Belgian company Beherman Demoen negotiated a licence to produce the APC in 1976. Their vehicle, put into production in 1982, was called the BDX Armoured Personnel Carrier. In total 123 of these were produced, 43 for the Belgian Air Force and 80 for the Gendarmerie. The design was then bought by Vickers who developed the vehicle further and called it the "Valkyr", but no further vehicles were sold.

## Timoney Mk V/BDX APC

**Country:** Eire (Republic of Ireland)
**Entered service:** 1982
**Crew:** 2 plus 10 infantry
**Weight:** 9,957kg/9.8 tons
**Dimensions:** Length – 4.95m/16ft 3in
　　Height – 2.75m/9ft
　　Width – 2.5m/8ft 3in
**Armament:** Main – 7.62mm/0.3in machine-gun
　　Secondary – Small arms
**Armour:** Maximum – 12.7mm/0.5in
**Powerplant:** Chrysler 8-cylinder 134kW/180hp petrol engine
**Performance:** Speed – 100kph/62mph
　　Range – 700km/430 miles

LEFT: **A Warrior at speed during training in the Gulf. The driver and vehicle commander have their hatches open. Crews of AFVs had to be taught how to drive in the desert so as not to create a dust cloud. On the rear of the vehicle is a large storage bin for personal equipment.** ABOVE: **One of the Warrior development vehicles. The vehicle is fitted with several clusters of four infrared and smoke screening dischargers. On the turret are a further four smoke dischargers on each side. The driver's entry hatch is mounted on the sloped side of the vehicle hull.**

# Warrior Mechanized Combat Vehicle

The British Army's FV 432 entered service in the 1960s and was due for replacement by 1985. Development of the MCV-80 as the replacement vehicle started with various studies being carried out between 1967 and 1977, when the detailed design work started. By 1980, three prototype vehicles were being tested and these were followed by a further seven vehicles which were completed in 1984. In the same year development of MCV-80 variants and derivative vehicles started. In 1985 GKN Defence Operations were awarded three contracts for 1,048 MCV-80 vehicles, and it was given the name "Warrior" by the British Army. Production started in January 1986, the first vehicle being produced in December 1986. The first batch of vehicles numbered 290, consisting of 170 section vehicles and 120 of the specialized vehicles. Once production started the British Army would take delivery of 140 vehicles per year, and 70 per cent of the 1,048 Warriors ordered would be section vehicles. Vickers Defence Systems manufacture the turret in a modular form ready to drop into a vehicle on the production line, while Rolls-Royce do the same with the engine pack which is made up of the engine, the transmission and the cooling system. The first three variants under development, the Infantry Command Vehicle, the Artillery Observation Vehicle and a Repair and Recovery Vehicle, were all completed in 1985. Unfortunately, the cost of the Warrior has meant that by 2004 it had still not fully replaced the FV 432.

The hull of the Warrior is of an all-welded aluminium construction, and is proof against small-arms fire and shell splinters. The driver is located in the front of the vehicle on the left-hand side, with a single large hatch over his position that is fitted with a wide-angle periscope which can be changed for a passive night-sight. The engine is next to the driver on the right-hand side and is a Rolls-Royce Condor. This is linked to a

ABOVE: **The RARDEN-armed turret is covered in camouflage netting. Modern camouflage netting helps hide the vehicle on the battlefield from infrared and other sensors that are now carried by modern reconnaissance aircraft. The headlight clusters are mounted on the leading edge of the glacis.**

Detroit Diesel automatic transmission with four forward and two reverse gears made under licence by Rolls-Royce. The Warrior is fitted with a full NBC system and night-fighting equipment.

The two-man turret is a steel construction mounted in the centre of the vehicle but slightly offset to the left of the centreline. The vehicle commander sits on the right-hand side of the turret, with the gunner on the left. The vehicle commander can also double as the infantry section leader and can debus with the troops. The turret is armed with a 30mm/1.18in L21A1 cannon and a coaxial 7.62mm/0.3in machine-gun. The cannon can fire single rounds, a burst of six rounds or a high rate of 80 rounds per minute, all spent shell

LEFT: **All the crew of this Warrior have their hatches open. The driver's side hatch has gone and the main driver's hatch can now open fully to the left. A Spartan CVR(T) is following close behind.**
BELOW: **A pair of Warrior vehicles on a live-firing range. The low height of the turret can clearly be seen from the instructor standing on the rear of the vehicle. On each side of the rear door on the back of the Warrior are large equipment storage containers. A wire-mesh storage box has been fitted to one of the roof hatches in the rear of the Warrior.**

cases being expelled outside the turret. However, there have been a few problems with the main gun, in particular with accidental discharge.

The troop compartment is at the rear of the vehicle and holds seven men, four on the right and three on the left-hand side of the vehicle, each man having his own seat and seat belt. There is no provision for the infantry to fire their weapons from inside the Warrior. The main entrance and exit for the infantry section is a single power-operated door with a vision port in it in the rear of the vehicle, and above the troop compartment is a large double hatch which, when opened, lies flat on the top of the vehicle. There are storage baskets on the rear of the vehicle for personal kit as there is insufficient room for this inside.

There are three different command versions of the Warrior – Platoon, Company and Battalion, the main difference between these vehicles being the communications equipment fitted.

The Warrior Repair and Recovery Vehicle has a 6,502kg/6.4-ton crane and a 20,015kg/19.7-ton capstan winch, and also a hydraulically operated ground anchor which allows the vehicle to pull 38,000kg/37.4 tons. Other vehicles of the Warrior family serving with the British Army are the Artillery Observation Vehicle and the Battery Command Vehicle. A desert version of the Warrior has been developed for the export market and this has been bought by Kuwait as the Warrior proved to be a very reliable vehicle during the Gulf War of 1991.

ABOVE: **This Warrior is on active service with British forces in Bosnia. It has been fitted with appliqué armour to the sides and front of the vehicle. The Warrior has proved to be a reliable and strong vehicle in combat.**

### Warrior Mechanized Combat Vehicle

**Country:** UK
**Entered service:** 1985
**Crew:** 3 plus 7 infantry
**Weight:** 24,486kg/24.1 tons
**Dimensions:** Length – 6.34m/20ft 10in
 Height – 2.79m/9ft 2in
 Width – 3.03m/9ft 11in
**Armament:** Main – 30mm/1.18in RARDEN cannon, and coaxial 7.62mm/0.3in machine-gun
 Secondary – Small arms
**Armour:** Classified
**Powerplant:** Perkins CV8 TCA 8-cylinder 141kW/190hp diesel engine
**Performance:** Speed – 75kph/47mph
 Range – 660km/412 miles

LEFT: **A 6x6 version of the VAB fitted with a Creusot-Loire TLi 52A one-man turret which is armed with a single 7.62mm/0.3in machine-gun.** ABOVE: **A basic 4x4 version of the VAB APC, as used by the French Army. All of the armoured shutters are in the open position on this vehicle. Behind the shutter the vision ports are protected by bullet-proof glass.**

# VAB Armoured Personnel Carrier

In the late 1960s the French Army issued a requirement for a wheeled APC, as the tracked AMX-10 was proving to be too expensive and complex to fill all the roles required of it. This was further extended in 1970 when a requirement for a Forward Area Control Vehicle (*Véhicule de l'Avant Blinde*, VAB) was identified. The French Army tested 4x4 and 6x6 versions between 1972 and 1974, eventually selecting the Renault 4x4 vehicle to fulfil both roles. Production started in 1976 and the first vehicles entered service in 1977.

The basic vehicle used by the French is the VAB VTT (*Véhicule Transport de Troupe*). Its hull is an all-welded steel construction, proof against small-arms fire and shell splinters, with an NBC system. The driver sits at the front of the vehicle on the left-hand side, with the vehicle commander/gunner beside him on the right. In front of them is a bullet-proof windscreen. Both have access doors in the side of the cab opening towards the front of the vehicle and hatches above their positions. The commander also has a machine-gun mount, the Creusot-Loire type CB 52, armed with a 7.62mm/0.3in machine-gun. This can be replaced with a TLi 52A turret or CB 127 12.7mm/0.5in gun and shield.

The engine compartment is behind the driver with the air intake and outlet in the roof. On the right-hand side of the vehicle is a passageway between the crew compartment and the troop compartment in the rear. The ten men in here sit on bench seats, five down each side, while the main access to the vehicle is via two doors in the rear of the VAB. There are two firing ports in each side of the vehicle and one in each door. The VAB is fully amphibious and is propelled in the water by two water jets.

Renault developed a 6x6 vehicle for the export market and offered both for sale. By 1999 the French Army had taken delivery of over 4,000 vehicles and over 700 (6x6 and 4x4 vehicles) had been sold to the export market. There are 13 different variations on the basic vehicle with various types of armament.

LEFT: **Several 6x6 and 4x4 VAB APCs taking part in a French Army exercise. The VAB in the front of the picture has been fitted with a basic ring mount over the roof hatch for a 12.7mm/0.5in heavy machine-gun. The cylinder below the gunner is the exhaust system for the vehicle.**

## VAB VTT

**Country:** France
**Entered service:** 1977
**Crew:** 2 plus 10 infantry
**Weight:** 13,614kg/13.4 tons
**Dimensions:** Length – 6.1m/20ft
   Height – 2.1m/6ft 11in
   Width – 2.5m/8ft 2in
**Armament:** Main – 7.62mm/0.3in machine-gun
   Secondary – Small arms
**Armour:** Classified
**Powerplant:** Renault MIDS 06.20.45 6-cylinder
   175kW/235hp diesel engine
**Performance:** Speed – 92kph/57mph
   Range – 1,000km/621 miles

LEFT: **This Shilka has the driver's hatch in the open position. In front of the driver's position is the splash board which helps to prevent water entering there. The main armament is at maximum elevation, and the Gun Dish radar is in the raised position at the rear of the turret.** BELOW: **A Shilka in travelling mode. The radar has been lowered and the guns brought down to the horizontal. To the left is a T-72 MBT and to the right is a BTR-60 PB, in the snow.**

# ZSU-23-4 Self-Propelled Anti-Aircraft Gun

In 1960 development started in the Soviet Union on a replacement for the ageing ZSU-57-2, which was too slow, inaccurate and did not have an all-weather capability. The replacement unit carries the Soviet designation *Zenitnaia Samokhodnaia Ustanovka* (ZSU), which mounts a 23-calibre armament (23mm/ 0.91in) of which there are four, hence ZSU-23-4. They also called it "Shilka" after the Russian river of that name. First seen during the 1965 November Parade, having entered service in 1964, its NATO reporting name is "Awl" but it is more popularly known as "Zoo-23". Production finished in 1983 with more than 7,000 vehicles being produced.

The hull and turret are an all-welded steel construction. The glacis plate is proof against small arms and shell splinters, but the turret is susceptible to shell splinter damage. The driver is located at the front of the vehicle on the left-hand side in a small cramped position, with the cold weather starter and battery compartment next to him on the right. His position can be fitted with infrared night-driving equipment. The other three members of the crew are positioned in the rear of the turret, the commander on the left-hand side with the other two beside him, and the guns are separated from the crew by a gas-tight armoured bulkhead. Access to the guns is via two large hatches in the front roof of the turret. The gun barrels are water-cooled, although this is not always satisfactory and when the gunner

releases the trigger the guns can still fire several more rounds. The gunner can select either single, twin or all four gun barrels to engage a target. At the rear of the turret is the Gun Dish Radar System which can be folded down into the travel mode when on the move. The engine is in the rear of the Shilka which is fitted with a full NBC system.

The Shilka proved to be a very effective system and during the Middle East War of 1973 it accounted for 31 out of 103 Israeli aircraft shot down. They normally operate in pairs placed 200m/656ft apart, and the vehicle can fire on the move but this decreases the accuracy by 50 per cent.

### ZSU-23-4 Shilka SPAAG

**Country:** USSR
**Entered service:** 1964
**Crew:** 4
**Weight:** 14,021kg/13.8 tons
**Dimensions:** Length – 6.29m/20ft 8in
    Height – 2.25m/7ft 5in
    Width – 2.95m/9ft 8in
**Armament:** Main – 4 x AZP-23 23mm/0.91in
    cannon
    Secondary – None
**Armour:** Maximum – 15mm/0.59in
**Powerplant:** Model V6R 6-cylinder 179kW/240hp
**Performance:** Speed – 44kph/27mph
    Range – 260km/160 miles

RIGHT: **The large ammunition magazine running down the side of the turret can be clearly seen. Above the driver's hatch is the very small vision port. The driver has a very poor field of vision when the hatch is closed.**

# Glossary

**AA** Anti-Aircraft.

**AAGM** Anti-Aircraft Guided Missile.

**AFV** Armoured Fighting Vehicle.

**AP** Armour-Piercing.

**APC** Armoured Personnel Carrier.

**APU** Auxiliary Power Unit.

**ARV** Armoured Recovery Vehicle.

**ATGM** Anti-Tank Guided Missile.

**ATGW** Anti-Tank Guided Weapon.

**bustle** Rear storage container on a vehicle.

**"buttoned up"** All hatches are shut with the crew inside.

**calibre** Diameter of the bore of a gun barrel.

**chain gun** Machine-gun.

**chassis** Running gear of vehicles: axles, road wheels etc.

**closed-down** All hatches are shut.

**coaxial** The secondary armament mounted to fire alongside the main armament.

**cupola** Domed turret fitted with vision devices, frequently for use of vehicle commander.

**CVR(T)** Combat Reconnaissance Vehicle (Tracked).

**double-baffle** Muzzle brake with two holes.

**ECM** Electronic counter measures.

**glacis** Defensive sloping front plate on an armoured vehicle.

**GPMG** General Purpose Machine-Gun, typically 7.62mm/0.3in calibre.

**HE** High-Explosive.

**HEAT** High-Explosive Anti-Tank.

**HE-FRAG** High-Explosive Fragmentation.

**HMG** Heavy Machine-Gun, typically 12.7mm/0.5in calibre.

**hull** The main body of the vehicle above the chassis.

**IFV** Infantry Fighting Vehicle.

**LMG** Light Machine-Gun, typically 7.62mm/0.3in calibre.

**LVTP** Landing Vehicle Tracked Personnel.

**mantlet** Protective covering for the hole in the turret where the main armament emerges.

**MBT** Main Battle Tank.

**MILAN** *Missile d'Infanterie Léger Anti-Char*.

**muzzle brake** Way of slowing down the recoil of the barrel by using the excess gases from the propellant charge.

**NBC** Nuclear, biological, chemical. Typically used when describing systems which offer protection against these threats.

**over-pressurization system/ over-pressure system** Air pressure in a vehicle is raised above outside atmospheric pressure as a crude form of NBC protection.

**pdr** Contraction of "pounder" – old British measurement for artillery pieces, which were measured by weight of their shell, e.g. "6pdr" – six-pounder.

**pistol ports** An opening in a vehicle allowing small arms to be used from inside.

**run-flat tyres** These can be driven on even after punctures for around 30km/18 miles.

**SAM** Surface-to-Air Missile.

**SAMM** Surface-to-Air Mobile Missile.

**section vehicle** A platoon commander's vehicle or a vehicle which can carry an infantry section of 10 men.

**SPAAG** Self-Propelled Anti-Aircraft Gun.

**spaced armour** Armour built in two layers with a space in between.

**SP ATGW** Self-Propelled Anti-Tank Guided Weapon.

**SPG/H** Self-Propelled Gun/Howitzer.

**standardized (of US vehicles)** Term used when a vehicle is accepted into service with the US Army and given a military designation.

**sustained rate of fire** Rate of fire which a gun-crew maintain over a period of time.

**TOW missile** Tube-launched, Optically-tracked, Wire-guided missile.

**track grousers** Attachments to tracks for extra grip over soft ground or ice.

**uparmoured** Increases in the original basic armour fitted to a vehicle.

**vision slits/slots** An opening in a vehicle fitted with a vision device.

**weapon station** Weapons firing position.

# Index

## Acknowledgements

The author would like to thank
David Fletcher, historian at the
Tank Museum, Bovington, and
his staff, the DAS MT Section,
Duxford, and the Cambridge
Branch of MAFVA, for all their
help and advice. A special thank
you to Bridget Pollard for all her
encouragement and help,
especially "de-jargoning".

The publisher would like to
thank the following individuals
and picture libraries for the use
of their pictures in the book.
Every effort has been made
to acknowledge the pictures
properly. However, we apologize
if there are any unintentional
omissions, which will be
corrected in future editions.
l=left, r=right, t=top, b=bottom,
m=middle, um=upper middle,
lm=lower middle

**Imperial War Museum
Photographic Archive:** 20m
(H 36442); 21ml (H 28755);
72tl (BL/74/113/2/5); 72tr
(BHQ/73/169/3/20); 72b
(BHQ/73/169/3/14); 75b
(HU 41939).
**Jack Livesey Collection:**
2; 6–7; 10; 12–15; 16b; 17tr;
17bl; 18–19; 20t; 21t; 21mr;
21b; 22mr; 23; 25tl; 25tr; 26–33;
35–6; 38–58; 59tl; 59b; 60–1;
62t; 62m; 63; 64tl; 64tr; 65–71;
74; 75t; 75m; 76–105; 107t;
107mr; 107b; 108–12; 113tl;
113tr; 114–19; 120b; 122tr;
123m; 123b; 124–5; 127–8.
**Tank Museum Photographic
Archive:** 16t; 17tl; 17br; 22ml;
22b; 24; 25mr; 25b; 34; 37; 59tr;
62b; 64b; 73; 106; 107ml; 113b;
120tl; 120tr; 121; 126.
**TRH Pictures:** 1; 3; 5; 8–9; 122tl;
122b; 123t.